THE PRINCIPAL THING

Why faith?

THE PRINCIPAL THING

Why faith?

T.G. WITHERSPOON

ASCENDANCY
PUBLISHING

The Principal Thing—*Why Faith?*
Published by Ascendancy Publishing
PO Box 1371
Wolfforth, TX 79382

ISBN 978-0-9983923-2-5

Printed in the United States of America
2017

Some names and identifying details have been changed to protect the privacy of individuals.

Butterfly Silhouette Designed by Freepik
Edited by Monica Sharman and Kristen Witherspoon
Cover and Interior Design by Kristen Witherspoon

TABLE OF CONTENTS

FOREWORD

It is a joy to endorse Terry Witherspoon's book, *The Principal Thing*! I've known Terry and his family for a number of years. He has been in many of my meetings across the nation. Terry has a wonderful hunger for the Presence of God.

Your life will be significantly blessed and enriched greatly by not only reading this book but truly studying and applying its teaching to your life. These are the most exciting times in human history; we must make the most of each moment (see Ephesians 5:14-18).

These are the days of harvest, and truly the fields are ripe and ready for reaping. Terry's book will help you grasp a better understanding of how to step out into the harvest field. Always remember we are not advancing alone; we have a constant companion—the Powerful Person of the Holy Spirit (see Acts 1:8).

Knowing that in Christ Jesus we are truly overcomers and victorious in every area of our life (see Romans 8:37), take your time as you read and ponder the principles of this timely book.

Bobby Conner
Eagles View Ministries

PREFACE

Are there people today who are doing the things Jesus did? The answer is yes! I personally know a man that has raised people from the dead. This man, Bobby Conner, has prayed for and seen many creative miracles. Many signs and wonders have been witnessed in his ministry all over the world.

Several years ago, Bobby was preaching in Mexico at a very large meeting. At one point, Bobby was standing near the stage when he looked up and saw a man walking toward him with a little girl in his arms. The little girl's face had not been fully formed. The left side of her face was essentially missing. You could see inside her mouth as her tongue hung to the side and saliva ran down her dress. With tears in his eyes, the father held his little girl up to Bobby for prayer. Bobby didn't need to speak Spanish to see what the father was asking for.

Immediately, Bobby had a vision. He could see the little girl a few years into the future as she was being tormented by classmates. Next, Bobby could see the girl in her teen years standing next to a busy downtown street. There was immense sadness in her face as she stood next to the busy street. Suddenly, the girl stepped into the path of a bus, which killed her instantly. Then Bobby found himself back at the meeting, standing in front of the father holding his little girl.

Bobby immediately began to ask the Lord, "What should I do?" The Lord spoke to Bobby, giving him instructions. Bobby then reached out his hand and began to move his thumb over the area of the girl's face that was not formed. As Bobby moved his thumb from one side to the next, flesh and skin instantly grew over the area until the girl's face was completely perfect!

The Lord then spoke to Bobby saying, "Do you know why I healed that girl?"

Bobby then said, "No, why did you heal her?"

The Lord replied, "Because I am a good God."

This is one of the most amazing testimonies I have ever heard. This happened in front of many people. Bobby is an example of someone who has committed himself to live by faith and serve God. What was impossible became possible. This testimony is a great example of what Jesus said in the Bible. All things are possible for anyone who can believe. Jesus also said that those who believe in Him will be able to do the things that He did. There are reports of other people around the world who are beginning to do the things Jesus did.

Bobby and his family have become very dear friends to me and my family. Much of what I have with God today is a direct result of Bobby and Carolyn Conner's ministry.

I humbly dedicate this little book to them for helping me and my family in times of real need. Bobby and Carolyn have poured so much into our lives over the years. I will be forever grateful to them. I am especially grateful to them for modeling Jesus to me. They have demonstrated what it means to live for Jesus by serving others.

In Him,
T.G. Witherspoon

In Dedication To:
My wife, Renee, and our children:
Joshua, Jacob, and Kristen
And
Bobby and Carolyn Conner

1

THE QUESTION IS

BEWARE OF FLYING MAMMALS

It was a very dark night on the open plains of West Texas. My family and I were driving home after visiting another town for the day. The lines on the narrow highway flashed by so quickly they looked like a single pulsating line. It seemed as though nothing existed outside the view of our headlights. We had a full day, and all was quiet in the van.

Then from the back of the van I heard, "Beware of flying mammals." Our thirteen-year-old son chuckled as he made the comment.

I looked at Renee and said, "What a funny comment." Within a few minutes I looked up to witness a startling scene unfolding before us. It seemed like it was playing in slow motion, even though it really happened in a flash.

I saw three large feral pigs crossing the road. They were huge! The three pigs looked into the oncoming headlights and began to move faster than pigs are known for. Two of the pigs immediately turned back. The third one decided to keep going forward. Our minivan hit this pig just the right way to send it soaring into the air. I can clearly remember seeing that pig as it slowly flew by my window. My wife screamed, "Go back and see if it's okay!"

I screamed, "No, if it's okay, then it's really mad!"

God had invaded our little world and released a word through our son. I had been experiencing many things out of the ordinary prior to that night. God had been trying to get my attention. We have since witnessed miraculous events and have seen many people supernaturally healed. What does supernatural mean? The Oxford Dictionary defines "supernatural" as "(of a manifestation or event) attributed to some force beyond scientific understanding or the laws of nature."

There is a life available to everyone where the supernatural becomes a part of their world. There is a way of living where nothing is impossible.

My two older brothers and I were raised by a single mother. It was a happy but very modest upbringing. I did manage to attend college and graduate with a degree in architecture. During that time I married Renee and worked at raising our family and building an architectural practice. We attended a mainline denominational church where I served as a deacon.

I began to have encounters that were difficult to explain. I became dissatisfied with the status quo. My Christian life was like living on a roller coaster, with moments of exhilarating highs and crushing lows. There was something missing in my religious experience. I was at the end of my rope after several years on the roller coaster. Then one day I had an encounter with the Holy Spirit similar to what is described in Acts, Chapter 2 in the Bible. Since then I have experienced a Christian life filled with power.

For several weeks I heard God say, "Faith is the principal thing." This happened numerous times. Finally, I posed a question to God: "God, why did You choose faith as the means to receive things from You?"

The Question:
"Why did God choose faith as the means to receive things from Him?"

As I understand the Bible, Heaven's economy is based on faith. Faith is like the money used to interact with Heaven. We can't please God or receive anything without faith. But with faith we can turn impossibilities into reality. We can literally obtain supernatural blessings from God.

Isaiah 55:1-2 NKJV

"Ho! Everyone who thirsts,
Come to the waters;
And you who have no money,
Come, buy and eat.
Yes, come, buy wine and milk
Without money and without price.
Why do you spend money for what is not bread,
And your wages for what does not satisfy?
Listen carefully to Me, and eat what is good,
And let your soul delight itself in abundance.

It may seem obvious to some, but I really wanted to know the answer. I mean, He is God, He could have set the whole thing up any way He wanted. God purposed in His mind to create everything, including mankind. He had to choose a means for us to interact with Him. He could have set up any number of methods for our obtaining His blessings or for entering into Heaven.

He could have based it on how strong we are, how smart we are, or how much we could do for Him.

Many religions teach their followers that they may gain a favorable eternal outcome based on such things. Some religions teach their followers that a good after-life depends on the quantity, quality, and method of the things they do during their lifetime. Others believe they will have a chance at a good afterlife if they are dominant over other religions. I admit this book is written from a Christian worldview.

Christianity is the only religion that is entirely faith-based, regardless of what people do or don't do (see Romans 3:28). In fact, Christianity is not really a religion at all. Being a Christian means that a person has a relationship with God through Jesus, by faith, that produces a new life within them. This new life will be pleasing to God.

Although I was genuinely curious about the answer, I believe that God had prompted me to ask the question so He could provide the answer. A few days later God suddenly began to answer me.

You may ask, how do you know it was God that was speaking to you? The same way I know my wife when she calls me on the phone. I know her voice and how she speaks to me from having a relationship with her.

After the answers began to flood in, I felt God tell me to put them in a book. I said to God, "I have never written a book." I was not an ordained minister and had never been to Bible college. It may seem unusual that God would want me to write a book about faith. It certainly seemed unusual to me. Nevertheless, that's just what happened. He gave me some principles and wanted me to write a book based on them.

I have come to believe that the insights the Lord gave me are the very secret to everything. The secret to a happy fulfilling life can be found in these truths. By happy fulfilling life, I mean coming into the realization of why we exist and then fulfilling that purpose.

In fact, these truths have the potential to shift the current thought paradigm in Western society—although many will disregard the information because they are confined to a worldview imposed upon them from an early age.

We are products of a highly educated and technologically focused worldview. And we have been conditioned to disregard anything not acknowledged by current scientific understanding. Anything that cannot be visually studied and observed in the natural sense is dismissed as having no real basis for truth.

However, some emerging fields today embrace the metaphysical aspects of our existence. Supernatural aspects that include the belief in forces and laws that originate from an unseen realm. The emergence of such theories reflects a universal awareness within people that there is more to our existence than what we can observe with our natural senses.

History and anthropology have clearly shown that man has related to a realm beyond the natural world from our earliest existence. It was only at the emergence of the modern age that societal forces began to pressure people to disregard anything pertaining to a spiritual existence.

The insights presented in this book can help people see a higher and nobler way of living. We can view the world around us in a fresh way and interact with a realm we don't see in the natural.

I believe God is desiring to reveal Himself to the world in this fresh way. Even though this book is mostly directed toward Christians, I hope that others will open their minds to a higher and nobler way of thinking.

2

WHAT'S THE BIG DEAL?

Jesus said to him, "If you can believe,
all things are possible to him who believes."
– Mark 9:23 (NKJV)

A PLACE FOR WILLIE

A few years ago my wife and I took our son to Dallas for a doctor's visit in one of the largest hospitals of the region. As we sat in the waiting area before the appointment, I became restless thinking about all the people we passed by coming into the building. Many patients sat outside trying to get a little sunshine. I told my wife and son that I was going outside to find someone to pray for and would be right back.

Immediately, I saw an elderly man sitting on a concrete bench. He was wearing the typical patient attire of robe and pajamas. He was staring down at the ground and leaning forward over the cane between his legs. Deep wrinkles marked his face, and his white hair glistened in the morning light. I struck up a conversation and asked if I could pray for him. He said his name was Willie and that there was something wrong with his neck and lungs, but he seemed reluctant to talk about it. I prayed for him anyway and asked the Lord to heal him. He said he felt better, but he continued to gaze downward, showing little interest.

I asked him what was really wrong. With tears in his eyes he explained that he was homeless. He had gotten used to sleeping in a clean bed and eating three meals a day, and now he was about to be discharged from the hospital. Pain engulfed his face from the thought of going back to the streets.

Immediately, I felt an unusually overwhelming compassion rising within my heart. I said, "Let's pray and ask Jesus to get you a place to stay." He just nodded without looking up. So I asked the Lord to find Willie a place to stay once he got out of the hospital and then went upstairs to rejoin my family.

We were on our way back downstairs within about twenty minutes. Once outside I could see that Willie was still sitting on the bench. He gazed downward and held a piece of paper with both hands. I introduced my family and then asked what he was holding. He looked up with a surprised expression and said, "You mean you don't know?"

I replied, "Know what?"

Willie explained that a young woman approached him soon after we prayed. She handed him a piece of paper with seven addresses. The woman then told Willie he could go to any of those addresses when he gets out, and he would be welcome to stay there. Willie had a place to stay!

According to Willie, she just appeared from the crowd next to the bus stop and walked right up to him. She gave him the slip of paper and then left the same way she came. Willie said he lost sight of her among the crowd. The mystery woman appeared almost immediately after we prayed and handed him the answer to his prayers.

How did this happen? No one could have overheard our earlier conversation and prayer. No one was close to us, and the noise from the street traffic was very loud. Was she a messenger sent from Heaven? It clearly was some type of encounter beyond natural circumstances.

Willie had a wonderful expression of joy and peace as he clutched the piece of paper. He knew that there was a God and that he was loved. This event impacted all of us that day. Willie had a dire need, and God immediately met that need in an unexpected and unexplained way. I believe that God moved a mountain for Willie that day. Nothing is impossible with God.

Jesus said that our prayers would be answered if asked in faith. He said even major obstacles could be moved out of our way if we asked without doubting.[1]

There is an account in the Bible where Jesus healed a young boy. The father brought the boy to Jesus because His disciples had not been able to heal him. The father said to Jesus, "... *if You can do anything, have compassion on us and help us.*" At this point Jesus said something amazing. Jesus replied, "*If you can believe, all things are possible to him who believes*" (see Mark 9:20-23 NKJV).

Jesus declared that with proper believing, there are no impossibilities for those who follow Him. This statement is astounding to me. It must be either true or false. Jesus said that faith could literally remove all natural limitations or obstacles in our lives. The idea of being able to live a life where nothing is impossible is worth investigating.

In the Gospel of John, Jesus declared that anyone who believes in Him will do what He did and even greater things.[2] If this statement is true, then there is a potential for tapping into a way of living that would be superhuman by any known standard. Jesus raised the dead, healed sick people, and performed all kinds of miracles. He walked on water and turned water into wine. He was able to pray over enough food to feed a few people and then see it supernaturally multiply into enough to feed thousands. The implication is truly breathtaking.

Chapter 6 in the Book of Acts describes some problems regarding how some people in the early church were being treated. The church leaders got together and directed the people to pick out seven men to take care of the problem. The men that were chosen had to have three minimum characteristics. They had to have a good reputation, be full of the Holy Spirit, and possess wisdom. The people selected seven men that met those qualifications.

All seven men were full of the Holy Spirit, reputable, and wise. And yet there was one that stood out. Stephen possessed something notable. He was "*full of faith and the Holy Spirit*" (Acts 6:5). The other six men were full of the Holy Spirit, reputable, and wise. But it was faith that distinguished Stephen from the other six.

Stephen is later singled out again. The Bible says he was "*full of faith and power*" and "*did great wonders*" *and signs among the people*" (Acts 6:8). Being full of faith and the Holy Spirit resulted in being full of "*faith and power.*" Faith and power resulted in "*great wonders and signs among the people.*" One man stood out because he possessed a faith that stood out. Stephen lived a life where nothing was impossible. Faith is the principal thing.

The truths contained in this book can be found in the Bible. And the potential to live a life without impossibilities is available to anyone willing to follow Jesus.

CAN YOU SEE?

One day we stopped to visit with a couple walking along the side of the road. We believed the Lord wanted us to pray for one of them. The man, whose name was Juan, had severe pain in his wrists due to working in a restaurant for more than twenty years. He could not move his wrists in the slightest direction without severe pain. We asked Jesus to heal him, and the pain immediately was gone! He was shocked as he moved his hands back and forth, flexing his wrists.

I looked into Juan's eyes and could see that he had cataracts. Both of his eyes were light gray. I asked if we could pray for his eyes, and he agreed. After a few seconds he opened his eyes. His wife was startled and screamed, "Your eyes are bright brown again!"

God had instantly dissolved the cataracts in Juan's eyes. His eyes went from cloudy gray to beautiful bright brown. He was stunned as he looked around saying, "I can see clearly again!"

God is doing the miraculous through His people all over the world. Someone may ask, if miracles really happen, why don't we see them reported in the news? Much of the world today is controlled by a system with an agenda. Miracles that testify to the truth of the Bible are not readily propagated by any of the current world systems. Popular media, news outlets, and major entertainment industries are not friendly to anything that would substantiate the Bible.

Unbelief is another reason miracles are not widely reported today. Many people, including Christians, have been conditioned to not believe. Others are afraid to admit they believe in the supernatural because they don't want to be labeled as weird or strange. Miracles are weird and strange by definition. Nevertheless, God is showing up and working miracles through His people.

If you follow Him, amazing promises are available

right now for you. Hundreds of promises from God to His people can be found throughout the Bible. Here are just a few:

We can live forever (see John 3:16).

We can be joined to God (see 1 Corinthians 6:17).

He forgives us (see Psalm 103:3).

He heals our diseases (see Psalm 103:3).

He delivers us from trouble (see Psalm 50:15).

He removes fear (see Psalm 27:1).

He will bless our finances (see Deuteronomy 28:12).

God has also attached a big "YES" to each promise. The Bible says that "*all the promises of God in Him are yes, and in Him amen, to the glory of God through us*" (2 Corinthians 1:20 NKJV).

Find a promise in the Bible. If you follow Jesus, the answer to that promise is yes and amen! It gives God glory to give you what He's promised. God's promises belong to anyone willing to accept His offer of salvation through Jesus. The greatest promise is that we can spend eternity with Him.

We have the promises and an answer of "YES." The question is, how do we access them? The Apostle Paul described many great things that were accomplished by those who came before us. He revealed the secret of how God's people obtained promises and performed supernatural exploits: "*through faith [they] subdued kingdoms, worked righteousness, obtained promises, stopped the mouths of lions, quenched the violence of fire, escaped the edge of the sword, out of weakness were made strong, became valiant in battle, turned to flight the armies of the aliens*" (Hebrews 11:33-34 NKJV).

The promise is there, the answer is "YES," and faith is the means to access it. The impossible became possible because of faith. Faith is the principal thing.

The Apostle John wrote about a promise of God that is almost impossible to believe. It's so amazing that I wouldn't have believed it if it wasn't in the Bible. John said, "*Now this is the confidence that we have in Him, that if we ask anything according to His will, He hears us. And if we know that He hears us, whatever we ask, we know that we have the petitions that we have asked of Him*" (1 John 5:14-15 NKJV). He said that we can ask for anything from God and if it's within His will, we get what we asked for.

John is not the only one to make that statement. Jesus said the same thing. Jesus declared that anyone who believes in Him would do what He did. And then

Jesus said that He would grant anything asked in His name. I like *The Message* version of the Bible for these statements:

John 14:12-13 MSG
The person who trusts me will not only do
what I'm doing but even greater things, because I,
on my way to the Father, am giving you the same work to
do that I've been doing. You can count on it.
From now on, whatever you request along the
lines of who I am and what I am doing, I'll do it.
That's how the Father will be seen for
who he is in the Son. I mean it.

Now this is truly a breathtaking statement! Jesus clearly said He would grant anything we ask for, as long as it was within God's will.

Imagine that God gave you a credit card with your name on it. This card has no expiration date and no credit limit. It's good at any location in the world, and it can be used to purchase anything as long as it's legal. The card can even purchase things that don't exist yet. And on this card would be a big, bold title across the top that says "FAITH."

We don't need more promises. We need to access what He has already made available.

So what is the big deal? Faith is the big deal. Faith is the principal thing required today. There are so many promises available for God's people. We don't really need more promises. We need to access what He has already made available.

- Your faith will grow
  and become powerful.

- You will obtain all
  of the promises of God.

- You will ask what you
  desire and He will grant it.

- You will live a life where
  nothing is impossible!

3

JEREMIAH AND THE CAT

I remember growing up in West Texas with my brothers. There was a special system for determining social status in our neighborhood. Having two older brothers meant that I wouldn't get picked on by any of the neighborhood bullies. My brothers were the only ones allowed to pick on me. This was how things were where we grew up. There was a natural order based on how big or how strong you were. Sometimes being the smallest meant not being chosen for a game of football.

In the world today many people are passed over by society because they don't measure up in some way. Many are discounted because they are not smart enough. Some are overlooked because of their race, height, or any other number of cultural biases.

Imagine a God that would only take the strongest or smartest people. All of the other people would be out of luck. They would be left to fend for themselves.

Survival of the fittest on a universal scale. A deity like that would be a cruel and unloving god. A god like that would be barbaric or animal-like in nature. This brings us to the first answer to why God made faith the currency of Heaven. Faith places children at the front of the line.

Answer #1
Faith places children at the front of the line.

Faith allows everything to be received as a little child. Jesus taught that you must change and become as a little child in order to enter the kingdom of God.[3]

Have you ever noticed that little children have an easy time believing in impossible things? Believing seems effortless to them. Adults have been taught to believe only what they can see. They have been conditioned to say, "Let me see, and then I will believe." But Jesus declared that if we believe, then we will see.[4] This requirement offends many people. This way of living seems unintellectual to some. However, as we will see, placing faith over intellectual understanding is actually a more noble way of living.

JEREMIAH AND THE CAT

One day I was driving with my daughter when we saw a cat lying in the middle of the road. The cat had been hit by a car. We went back to see if there was anything we could do. It was bleeding from its head, and it was obvious that the cat was messed up. It seemed to look around blindly as we consoled it. It was struggling but could not stand.

We rolled the cat onto my daughter's old sweater and dragged it to the side of the road. Then a young boy, maybe nine years old, came running up and stood next to us. He asked, "What are y'all doing?"

I said, "We moved the cat off of the road so that it could die in peace."

The little boy, whose name was Jeremiah, said, "I know this cat! This cat belongs to the people across the street from me."

I was suddenly inspired to say, "I believe Jesus will heal this cat if we asked Him to."

Then Jeremiah looked up with his eyes wide open and exclaimed, "Yes!"

The three of us knelt down and asked Jesus to please heal the cat. Immediately the cat tried to stand up! We then carried the cat to its home, and it started running around as though nothing had happened at all. We saw Jeremiah a few days later, and he told us that the cat was fine.

This is a wonderful example of childlike faith. Jeremiah was not worried about natural limitations, what people might think, or what it would mean if we prayed and nothing happened. He was instantly willing to believe for the impossible. Jeremiah was a smart kid, but he did not let intelligence become a limitation. The devil is always trying to get people to be reasonable.

The devil is always trying to get people to be reasonable.

Do you remember what it was like to be a child? It's meant to be a time filled with wonder and hope. Remember when it was easy to dream about the future with hope? We could be carefree because we were being cared for. Looking back at our childhood can seem like such a long time ago. As adults, our lives become weighed down with burdens and fears. For many people, life has become like a bad dream.

Imagine the following bad dream—endless lines of cars on a highway six lanes wide. People sitting in bumper-to-bumper traffic as far as the eye can see.

Horns blaring and people yelling out of their windows. Anger and anxiety filling the air like exhaust rising above the road. Now see an exit ramp opening up before you. That exit ramp is Faith.

Faith is the exit that leads to wide-open spaces and spectacular views. Faith offers the option for you to be childlike again and gives you the ability to be optimistic. You will be able to dream again and live a life without limitations.

God has made it so easy enter into Heaven and receive things from Him. Even very small children can receive as much as the strongest and smartest among us. God is so inclusive and fair that He wants everyone to have easy access to His blessings. He doesn't want anyone left out. God has set things up in a way that gives everyone a chance to receive His love and blessings.

Faith provides a higher, nobler means for interacting with God. It is a system of interacting with Him that removes all natural limitations that people may have. Faith is not dependent on a person's IQ level, strength, size, age, or any other limitation. Faith takes all that God has to offer and makes it available to everyone without exception.

You may not be able to lift 500 pounds, but you

can believe. You may not be able to solve differential equations, but you can believe. You may not have come from a rich family, but you can believe. You may not be young anymore, but you can believe. The physically weak and the world-class athlete are made equals in the arena of faith.

Faith declares that everyone is equal in God's eyes and has equal access to Him. Here is another answer to my question. Faith declares that every single person is precious to God.

Answer #2
Faith declares that every single person is precious to God.

Faith places value on the individual in God's eyes and gives access to all of Heaven's blessings to that person apart from the masses. In the economy of faith, the individual is elevated to a position of great importance and significance. It does not matter where you are from or what your family history is.

A life based on faith is a far nobler and higher way to live. World systems are almost always contrary to these principles. For example, only the rich and powerful can gain access to world leaders. The elderly and imperfect are considered to have less value in some societies. And some religions make women second-class citizens. Other religions say that individuals are not important compared to the whole. Yet with Biblical faith every single individual can gain direct access to God. Faith declares that you are precious to God.

I SEE YOU

One day I was driving around a low-income apartment complex. We often would drive around as the Lord directed us. I turned a corner near the alley and saw a lady limping as she carried her trash to a dumpster. Her name was Otelia. She said, "I have thyroid cancer, my throat is swollen, and I can't swallow very good." She had pain all over, and it hurt her just to walk.

I prayed and asked Jesus to heal her. She instantly screamed, "I felt something jump out of my throat! My throat opened up!" She ran around crying as she said, "All the pain is gone from my body! I can swallow and breathe now!" Otelia then showed me a lump on her wrist that caused a lot of pain. It appeared to be carpal tunnel. We asked Jesus to heal it, and the lump and pain left. She said, "I work at the school kitchen, and now I will be able to roll the tortillas again!"

This woman had been in a very difficult place in her life. She was in pain, in a bad relationship, and on the verge of becoming homeless. But suddenly Otelia was filled with joy and hope because God had seen her near the trash dumpster. Faith declares that every single person is precious in God's eyes.

What is faith from a Biblical point of view? According to the definition used for the original language in the New Testament, faith can be described as "a firm persuasion." To have faith in someone means to trust them.

When my children were little, they were always very interested in what I had to say. They believed me when I told them that the large animal next to the road was a cow. They believed me because they knew me. They trusted me because they knew I would tell them the truth. They trusted me even though they didn't understand everything. They were satisfied with the answer because I was their dad and they knew that I loved them.

This delighted me as their dad. Similarly, believing that He is God and that He desires to reward us pleases our Heavenly Father.

According to the Bible, we cannot please God without faith. The Bible also says that there are two things we must believe in order to please God. First, we must believe that He exists. Second, we must believe that He loves us enough to respond and reward us when we seek Him.

Getting to know God as your Dad is key to growing in childlike faith.

That's right. You can please God by believing that He is God and that He wants to reward you. Let that sink in for a moment… It pleases God when you believe He wants to reward you. Getting to know God as your Dad is a key to growing in childlike faith.

Hebrews 11:6 NKJV
But without faith it is impossible to please Him, for he who comes to God must believe that He is, and that He is a rewarder of those who diligently seek Him.

- You have faith in God.

- You believe God is leaning
  forward and yearning
  to bless you.

- You find joy and a sense of
  wonder in life again.

- You are set free to dream again.

- You live a life where
  nothing is impossible!

4

I WANT YOU TO WANT ME

According to the Bible, God wants us to believe He is God and He deeply desires to bless us. In other words, He wants us to think properly about who He is and that He desires to have a relationship with us. Since we know that God wants to have a relationship and that this is achieved by faith, we can view faith as the contact point with God.

The heart is used as a symbol in the Bible. The heart represents the mind, will, and emotions of a person. The valentine symbol has been used as a visual representation of the heart in many cultures.

As an illustration, picture the valentine symbol. Now picture a symbol within that valentine. Imagine the symbol inside the valentine is a spiritual organ called "Faith." For understanding's sake, we can view faith as a spiritual organ inside the heart. This faith organ provides the point of relationship with God.

So how does this spiritual organ give us a relationship with God? Some Biblical context is needed before answering that question. In the beginning, God created Adam and Eve. (For the sake of conversation, when I mention Adam, I mean Adam and Eve or all of mankind.) He placed them in a garden east of a place called Eden. This paradise is referred to as the Garden of Eden (see Genesis, Chapter 1).

Within that garden were two trees. One of the trees was called the *Tree of the Knowledge of Good and Evil* and the other was called the *Tree of Life*. God had instructed them to eat freely from everything in the garden except for the fruit of the *Tree of the Knowledge of Good and Evil*. That fruit was forbidden.

Adam and Eve were in perfect relationship with their Creator. To remain in paradise, they only needed to obey a single command. Unfortunately, the devil convinced them to eat from the forbidden tree. This act brought death to man and decay into the world, just as God had previously warned them. That disobedience separated Adam from God.

Adam's choice was a crime against God. Any common understanding of justice reveals that when a crime is committed within a society, a debt is owed. That society would not be just if crimes could be committed without a cost. The scales of justice are balanced after a debt has been paid. God is just, and therefore, crimes against Him come with a price. Everyone comes into the world with Adam's debt and with his fallen nature.

So why does everyone born after Adam have the same spiritual debt? When Adam and Eve ate from the *Tree of the Knowledge of Good and Evil* they gained an awareness of what was right and wrong. They suddenly had a conscience. They knew they had disobeyed God. The Bible says every person is accountable for what they know or have.[5] Where much is given… much is required. Adam suddenly knew the difference between good and evil but could not live up to the knowledge he had. He was now accountable for what he knew. This presented a spiritual debt that he was unable to pay. He was now separated from God.

During creation God made everything to reproduce "*according to its kind.*" Adam ceased being one kind of man and became another kind after rebelling against God. His position in creation had changed.

Adam could only reproduce after his own kind from that time forward. Therefore, everyone born since Adam comes into the world different from God's original intent. People are born into the world with a conscience prompting them to know right from wrong. And since everyone has a conscience, this knowledge of good and evil, they are accountable for it.[6] That's why everyone is guilty and has a debt they cannot pay. Everyone starts out spiritually separated from God and unable to be good. This means everyone starts out under judgment.

God was not going to allow His original plan for man to be permanently derailed by the devil. God had a plan to restore things.

The Creator sent part of Himself, His Son Jesus, to the earth from Heaven more than two thousand years ago. A young Hebrew woman named Mary gave birth to Jesus after supernaturally getting pregnant by the Holy Spirit. Jesus lived as a man and yet lived without doing anything contrary to God's moral requirements.

Adam and Eve had been created to express God's image before failing. Jesus came to the earth and perfectly expressed God's image. Jesus came to be like a second Adam in order to reverse what the first Adam had done.[7] Jesus completely understood God's standards and yet could live up to them perfectly. Therefore, He was the only one who could pay the price for everyone. He did this by dying on the cross.

God declared that He would forgive anyone who believed Jesus died for them. God attributes the perfection of Jesus to you when you believe. Jesus took all of your punishment, and you get all of His benefits. God is offering to let everyone become born again. Jesus is now reproducing after His own kind on the earth. He is the firstborn among many brothers.

When we believe in Jesus, God places His Spirit into us and begins to manifest His life in us. We can only obtain a restored relationship with Him through faith in His Son Jesus.

God put a system of believing in place as the means to receive everything from Him. The Bible says that God has given everyone a measure of faith.[8] Every single person has been given a faith organ from God. Salvation is a gift that is received by faith.[9] Because it came from God, the faith you have is not your own. Everyone comes into the world with faith so that they might be restored to Him. God provided the sacrifice and supplied the means to believe for it.

What if we could contribute anything with regards to our being reconnected to God? This would mean that He would owe us. But God has provided everything for our salvation. No one will be able to say that God owes them. He remains the source of everything good.

Faith within our heart is the contact point where we can be joined with God. He greatly desires to have a relationship with us, and this is achieved through faith. This leads to the third answer to my question of why God made faith the currency of Heaven. Faith requires a relationship with God.

Answer #3
Faith requires a relationship with God.

If God had made our access to Him based on something besides faith, it would not necessarily require that we have a relationship with Him. For instance, suppose that the economy of Heaven was based on how much we could learn about Him. A smart person could learn facts about God then gain access to Him without having to know and love Him.

Many people see God as a stoic and impersonal figure that exists in some faraway place. However, the Bible portrays God as someone we can personally relate to. We can see throughout the Bible that He is capable of feeling similar emotions that we experience. God can be grieved, He can have joy, He can become angry, and He can become jealous.

We are created in His image, so it makes sense that we could relate to Him.

Jesus is the only begotten Son of God.[10] So what does it mean to be *"the only begotten Son of God?"* This means that Jesus was not created. Jesus proceeded from God. Jesus came into the world in the form of a man, but He was and still is God. Jesus said if you have seen Him, you have seen the Father. He related to people on very personal levels, and the Father desires to relate to us as well.

I remember a few years ago hearing a celebrity talking about how they decided not to follow the God of the Bible. This person made the decision because God described Himself as jealous. This well-known person declared that she would not worship a jealous God. The Bible does say in the book of Exodus that He is jealous. This declaration is made in the second commandment given to Moses on Mount Sinai.[11] There are several other instances in the Bible where God is described as jealous.

I can see how this might be a problem for that celebrity. It would be a problem if one views jealousy negatively. However, I believe that celebrity had a wrong understanding about the nature of God. This resulted in a misunderstanding. Does jealousy in that context reflect a good or bad trait?

Suppose that God is the very source of love. The Bible says that God is love.[12] Now suppose that God loves people in a measure that cannot be completely understood in human terms. God's love compels Him to feel jealous at the very thought of our giving affections to any other god besides Him. When God says that He's jealous, it's an attempt to help us understand the level of passion He feels.

If God were not jealous it would mean that He is only semi-interested in us. I would doubt the depths of someone's love for me if they didn't express jealousy when I turned to another.

Relationship with God produces a faith that is healthy and vibrant.

The point here is that we are created to have a relationship with God on a very personal level. We are created to relate to Him with similar emotions shared between us. Relationship with God produces a faith that is healthy and vibrant.

I WANT YOU TO WANT ME

One day I was driving near my office when I saw a prostitute walking along the road. She was a pretty woman wearing a dress and high heels. But she was limping and walking with a cane. I could see that she was in pain with each step she took.

There was an intense feeling within me that God wanted me to go back and pray for her. I walked up to her, introduced myself, and asked what her name was.

"Victoria," she said. I told her I believed that God wanted me to pray for her. Immediately, her face expressed disappointment.

I asked why she was limping. She said she had been in a car accident the previous week. Her hips and pelvic bones had been injured and pushed out of place. She couldn't walk without a cane and severe pain.

I put my hand on her shoulder and asked Jesus to heal her. Large tears immediately began to roll down her cheeks as she wept. I asked, "What's going on?"

Almost screaming, she said, "I can feel my bones moving into place!" Within seconds the Lord had totally healed her! She walked around in circles while shaking her head and holding up the cane.

She turned around and said, "Why would He do that?"

I said, "Oh, that's easy. He healed you because He loves you."

Victoria said, "But I just smoked crack cocaine fifteen minutes ago. Why would He do that?"

I replied, "Yes, but He loves you!"

We were created to interact with God on a personal level. The Bible declares that Jesus is coming for His people. This is represented by an analogy of a groom and bride coming together for marriage. Since faith requires a relationship, and a relationship requires fidelity, we can conclude that a healthy faith is dependent on fidelity with God. God said that He will be faithful to us and desires that we be faithful to Him.[13]

Faith without relationship becomes presumption.

Many people have tried to approach God strictly on a legal basis. They approach Him under the theological terms of having covenant with Him. It's true that we initially come into relationship with Him through a covenant. This legal agreement is His offer of redemption through Jesus. We accept and believe His offer which legally binds us to Him. However, it's not His desire that we would only maintain a legal relationship. Faith without relationship becomes presumption. The legal connection that gives us access to Him is supposed to grow into a relationship based on mutual love. We are to love Him because he first loved us.[14]

Sometimes people try to interact with God as

though He were a slot machine. Simply put in a coin and pull down the handle. If we are lucky we will hit the jackpot. But God has made faith the currency of Heaven because it requires a relationship.

Just like your physical organs need to be healthy to function properly, your faith organ must also be healthy. Our faith becomes stronger as our relationship with Him grows. The stronger our faith becomes, the more we walk in a life of His blessings.

Our faith is connected to our relationship with God because our faith came from Him. Faith is the contact point with God. As we grow closer to Him, our faith gets stronger and stronger. As we yield to Him, we come to know Him more intimately. We gain an experiential knowledge of His love for us and His desire to bless us. The growth and well-being of this faith organ depends on our having a relationship with God.

When someone sins against God, they weaken their faith.[15] It's as though the spiritual organ inside their heart gets bruised or wounded. When we damage our faith we hinder our ability to secure God's promises for our lives. The Bible says, "*Keep your heart with all diligence, For out of it spring the issues of life*" (Proverbs 4:23 NKJV). God is holy. Our hearts draw away from God when we rebel against Him.

A person can continue to rebel against God for so long that they eventually become estranged in their heart towards Him.[16] But He has placed his Holy Spirit into His people. When someone fails God or rebels against Him, the Holy Spirit works to convince the person that they need to change their direction.

The Bible says that if a person will agree with the Holy Spirit at these times, then God will quickly forgive the person.[17] Not only will God quickly forgive them, but He will also purge them of whatever is contrary to God.

This is not necessarily an issue of salvation. A relationship requires participation from both parties. Turning back to God is the remedy available to us when we have a weakened faith because of drawing away from God in our heart.

1 John 1:9 NKJV
If we confess our sins, He is faithful and just
to forgive us our sins and to cleanse us
from all unrighteousness.

Imagine having a fight with your spouse. After a little time, you both calm down and the anger subsides. But you say, "Don't expect me to apologize or say I love you. I gave my vows when we got married, and that should be good enough." That approach would not produce a very close relationship.

God sees our obedience as an expression of love toward Him. Jesus said, "*If you love Me, keep My commandments*" (John 14:15 NKJV). If God has told us to obey Him, it must be that He is offering the means to achieve the command. The Apostle Paul wrote, "*For with the heart one believes unto righteousness, and with the mouth confession is made unto salvation*" (Romans 10:10 NKJV). It's by faith that we will be able to keep God's commandments. One is an outgrowth of the other.

Since God desires a relationship and this is achieved through faith, what may we conclude? It's clear that He will strengthen your faith when you draw near to Him. As you live a life of faith in God, He will change your heart and this will produce obedience to Him. God will see your obedience as an expression of love. Your outward actions will match the love in your heart for Him.

It's God's love for us, not religious activity, that activates and energizes our faith, which produces His life in us.

Galatians 5:6 NKJV
For in Christ Jesus neither circumcision
nor uncircumcision avails anything,
but faith working through love.

Here is the outline of his plan:

- **God wanted relationship.**
- **God gave us faith.**
- **Faith requires relationship.**
- **Relationship produces more faith.**
- **More faith produces obedience.**
- **Obedience expresses love toward Him.**
- **Loving Him produces a good relationship.**

1 John 4:16-19 NKJV
And we have known and believed the love that
God has for us. God is love, and he who abides in love
abides in God, and God in him. Love has been perfected
among us in this: that we may have boldness in the day of
judgment; because as He is, so are we in this world. There
is no fear in love; but perfect love casts out fear, because
fear involves torment. But he who fears has not been made
perfect in love. We love Him because He first loved us.

Turning to God in faith means that we respond to
His love for us. God is the initiator. We are always re-

sponding to God's love for us. It's His faith working through His love.

This leads us back to the illustration of the faith organ within the heart of every person. Everyone comes into the world with one of these faith organs from God.

We become a new person spiritually once we use this faith to believe God's plan for saving us. God places His Spirit into us and begins the process of making us like Jesus. It's God's original intent that every man and woman be recreated in His image. This means He wants us to be like Jesus in how we think, act, and relate to Him.

Many have declared that faith is no longer relevant. We should remember what it really means. It means that God loves you with a passion beyond comprehension. It means that God deeply wants a personal relationship with you. Your faith was given to you from God. It's your very own. It's your ticket to a life without impossibilities.

John 15:13 NKJV
Greater love has no one than this,
than to lay down one's life for his friends.

Faith is the currency of Heaven. God put a system

in place that would only effectively work when someone comes into a relationship with Him. The deeper the relationship, the more powerful the faith.

- You will have a personal, intimate relationship with God.

- God's love will arise in your heart.

- You will draw near to Him, and your faith will become vibrant and strong.

- You will increasingly experience His Presence.

- You will live a higher, more noble life where nothing is impossible!

5

GOD IS PRO CHOICE

God had originally placed man on the earth with a divine purpose. That purpose was to have a relationship with Him and to have dominion over the earth. Adam was in perfect relationship with God. There was only one rule to obey. He said they could eat anything in the garden except the fruit from the *Tree of the Knowledge of Good and Evil*, the forbidden tree. Obedience to that one rule meant they would remain in paradise.

They were without the knowledge of good or evil. They had dominion over everything on the earth, including the demonic influences. They did not have the experience of sin. They were free to make the correct choice.

The Bible says that the forbidden tree was desirable. You can imagine the scene. Adam and Eve must have walked by the two trees many times. You can imagine they thought, "Wow that fruit looks really good.

I wonder what it tastes like? No, I choose to obey God. I will not eat from that tree." They chose to obey each time they walked past the forbidden tree.

The tree was very attractive to Adam and Eve. Forbidden things are often attractive. If the tree had been ugly or foul smelling, there really wouldn't have been much of a choice. God had created a scenario that declared, "You must choose." From the very beginning, they had a choice and they were able to choose.

God did not want to create little robots that He could wind up and turn loose just to watch them mindlessly declare, "I love God, I love God." They were created to rule and reign on the earth. They were created to reflect God's image. They were created to choose.

They had to choose to remain in relationship with Him. God has always desired a relationship with man. And any true relationship requires free will from both parties. Free will cannot exist without the element of choice. Adam and Eve made their choice when they ate from the forbidden tree.

Adam and Eve had to choose to obey. Today we must to choose to believe. We choose to believe so that we can be restored into fellowship with God. Here is another answer to my question: Faith requires choice.

Answer #4 - Faith requires choice.

I've always been fascinated with computers. It's amazing how a software programmer can create a language and then digitally imprint that language onto a computer's hard drive. This language dictates all of the computer's possibilities and limitations.

In a similar way, after we are reconnected with God, He begins to reprogram our hearts. We become one with Him as we surrender to Him through faith. This believing will produce obedience. This obedience is the result of our hearts being synchronized with Him. It's as if He writes His code on our heart's hard drive. This is an ongoing process. As we use our faith to surrender to Him, He writes the code and we by faith choose to follow.

Many people today believe they are helpless to change. They don't believe they can follow God's standards for living. Some make the argument, "I was born this way, I can't help it." Others say, "I have no choice. This is how God made me."

The truth is, all people are born "this way." Everyone comes into the world with Adam's nature. Every person is predisposed to live contrary to God. Some may have a predisposition to lie, others for addiction to substances, and still others for sexual perversions. Everyone is predisposed to disobey God's moral standards. In the face of greater sin, God has promised to provide more power and grace.[18] God will overcome evil with good. People won't get a pass just because they have a more difficult issue to overcome.

You can choose to accept God's offer. He has offered to forgive you. He has offered to change your heart. We are called to be holy because God is holy.[19] Since God has given the command, we can conclude that He will provide the way to achieve it. The way is through faith. It's God's desire to make everyone like Jesus in nature.

HANGING WITH A FRIEND

I was visiting a friend who managed a small rental store in another town. I felt led to pray for Sam, one of his employees. Sam was hesitant to believe in Jesus as his Savior. I told him Jesus loved him with an everlasting love and was still doing miracles for people today. I said, "You can go home tonight and ask the Lord to prove Himself to you." Then I said, "Maybe someone will come in that needs to be healed so you can see how Jesus works."

About five minutes later a lady named Maria came

in to pay her bill. The Lord revealed to me that her right hip needed to be healed. She wasn't speaking English, so I asked my friend to ask if her right hip was hurting. She instantly turned to look at me and said, "How did you know?!"

I said, "Jesus told me, and He is going to heal you." I asked Jesus to heal her, and then all the pain left her hip, back, and knees!

She said, "I could feel the bones moving and a buzzing in my ears!"

Maria told us about her relationship with God and how she had struggled to believe in Him. She said, "One day I finally asked Him to prove Himself to me, and He did." This really amazed Sam, who had witnessed the whole encounter. God demonstrated Himself to Sam and Maria.

The Bible says that if we honestly search for God, we will find Him. He desires to be found. If we truly humble ourselves and turn to Jesus, He will answer.

When someone says they have no choice, they have made their choice. They have chosen to refuse God's offer to set them free. Everyone has a choice and everyone makes a choice.

God has promised to deliver people from anything

that binds them. We must believe He will do this, just as we must believe He will heal or save us. People must believe it to receive it. He can and will do it—only believe.

What happens when someone comes to God through Jesus? He declares that the person is forgiven and perfect! The Apostle Paul wrote, "*For by one offering He has perfected forever those who are being sanctified*" (Hebrews 10:14 NKJV). When you choose to accept His offer, He assigns the righteousness of Jesus to you. You become a work in progress on earth, but you are considered perfect in Heaven.[20] God begins to make what's true about you in Heaven a reality on earth.

Jesus showed His followers how to pray. He prayed, "*Your kingdom come. Your will be done On earth as it is in Heaven*" (Matthew 6:10 NKJV). God is bringing Heaven to earth. He is aligning everything on the earth with Heaven, and that includes you. Your position is settled as you continue to follow and believe Him.

Consider the following scenario. A rich Benefactor says he is sending you to college to get a degree. He's going to pay for everything you need. There will be classes and tests along the way. It won't always be easy, but it will bring a great reward that will last forever.

He will walk next to you, helping with every task. Then the Benefactor says, "By the way, before you get started, here is your diploma and graduation ring." You unroll the diploma and see your name. It says you graduated with honors! Then your Benefactor says, "Now let's get started!"

God knows your struggles. He is offering to pay the way. He is waiting for everyone to choose Him.

God has always followed a simple pattern when He wants to provide something. First, God sovereignly provides a revelation. Secondly, the person sees and believes the revelation. Thirdly, the person receives what had been revealed. Everything we receive from Him follows this pattern:

1) Something is revealed;

2) the revelation is believed; and

3) the thing is obtained.

This pattern presents a choice in step number two. Faith requires the component of choice. We must choose to believe. There must be the option to not believe. The choice is our part.

The familiar story of the woman at the well illustrates this three-step process (see John 4:7-14). Jesus initiates a conversation with her because He intends to reveal something. He asked her for a drink of water.

It was unusual for a Hebrew man to be speaking to a Samaritan woman in a one-on-one encounter. The woman asked Jesus why He would speak to her. Jesus gave her a very interesting response. He said, *"If you knew the gift of God, and who it is who says to you, 'Give Me a drink,' you would have asked Him, and He would have given you living water."*

We see in this statement the three steps God uses to get things to us. In essence Jesus said, *"If you knew, then you would ask, and I would give."* She saw the revelation and believed. This believing prompted her to ask for what had been revealed. She then received it for herself. The woman later led many people from her village to believe as well.

You can see throughout the Bible, time and time again, where God revealed Himself to people and presented a choice. God took the children of Israel out of the bondage of Egypt. They were called to carry the message of God's coming atonement to the world. In the book of Deuteronomy, God reminded them of all that they had been through. Then God gave His standards for living in holiness. He presented a choice to them. He said, *"I call heaven and earth as witnesses today against you, that I have set before you life and death, blessing and cursing; therefore choose life, that both you and your descendants may live*" (Deuterono-my 30:19 NKJV). He called on them to choose life or death, blessing or judgment. They were free to choose.

We know from reading further that the children of Israel failed many times. So God instituted a system of service and sacrifices. If they followed the system of rituals, He would forgive them. All of the rituals and animal sacrifices were a way to cover their sins. But more importantly, the sacrifices and rituals were pointing to the final sacrifice of Jesus. God never intended for man to have a legal relationship with Him. God was moving toward the solution that would provide the kind of relationship He desired.

The Bible says that "*faith comes by hearing, and hearing by the word of God*" (Romans 10:17 NKJV). The original meaning for the term "word" expresses something that is uttered or spoken. This gives us a picture of God whispering in our ear—like suddenly getting a revelation from Him. This current word spoken to us from God causes our faith to grow.

When we get a revelation from Him, we have been presented a choice: to believe or not to believe. This choice will determine whether or not we receive what is revealed.

The Bible is a collection of writings accumulated over centuries. These writings were written by various people over time as they allowed themselves to become vessels of God's Spirit. In other words, God wrote the Bible through men. So when someone reads the Bible, they are reading truths spoken by God! That's a big deal. God can make those written words come alive to the person as they read. This is also a revelation. It becomes a current expression of what He is saying that causes faith to grow. Again a choice is presented. Get the revelation. Believe it. Then have it.

The apostle Paul wrote about faith working in a mighty way as a result of hearing God's truth.[21] Paul emphasized the point that amazing miracles are performed through God's people because they believed His message of salvation, not because they were striving to obey the commandments.

Galatians 3:5 MSG
Answer this question: Does the God who lavishly provides you with his own presence, his Holy Spirit, working things in your lives you could never do for yourselves, does he do these things because of your strenuous moral striving or because you trust him to do them in you?

Miracles happen when the Holy Spirit and faith

abide together. People choose to believe while in the Presence of God. We are restored to God by believing. We continue to live through Him the same way—by believing. We get the revelation of what He has said. We make the choice to believe God.

Again suppose that God had made the currency of Heaven something other than faith. Let's say that our reconnecting with Him was based on how smart we were. Our coming to God would be based on something outside of our control. Each person's intellectual ability is given at birth. This would mean that the choice would have been made for them. The removal of choice removes the possibility of a meaningful relationship.

Now let's suppose that Heaven's currency was only based on how much we could do for God. We could choose to throw our entire lives into doing things for Him. Although this scenario contains the component of choice, the element of relationship would not be necessary. So we can see that faith requires a choice that is dependent on a relationship.

This is a beautiful aspect of faith. The removal of choice would exclude any meaningful relationship. The removal of relationship removes the chance for a meaningful choice. Would we really want to have a relationship with a God that would force us to love Him?

Reflecting the image of our Creator requires the ability to choose.

Remember that God greatly values your ability to choose because He deeply desires a relationship with you. He wants you to be restored to a place on earth that is aligned with His original design. This includes walking in authority and dominion. God had originally desired that mankind reflect His image. Reflecting the image of our Creator requires the ability to choose. You have the power to choose.

JUAN CHOOSES

It was a hot summer day in West Texas. I was driving through a lower-income neighborhood when I looked up and saw a man riding on a mobility scooter. I knew the Lord wanted me to talk with him. He had a strange expression of fear on his face as I approached. He said, "My name is Juan. You can call me Johnny." I told him about Jesus and asked if he wanted to receive Him. Johnny quickly nodded yes! A cool wind swirled around us as we prayed.

I asked, "Why are you riding this scooter?"

He said, "I can't walk." He had been injured as a little boy some forty years earlier. He was in the back seat of the family car when it was hit by a train. The accident killed his dad who was driving and paralyzed the left side of Johnny's body.

I put my hands on his head and asked Jesus to heal him. The cool wind returned. Johnny said, "I could feel tingling inside my head!"

I said, "Move something you couldn't move before."

His eyes got big as he moved his left foot a little. He said, "I couldn't do that before!"

I got his address and said I would check on him later.

The following week I went to see him. Johnny was able to walk to the door! He was very happy and said he couldn't have done that before. My family and I prayed for Johnny several times after that. Johnny is able to walk now and can use his left arm and hand. We even saw him stand on his toes for the very first time. Johnny is still being restored, but when he goes somewhere he is walking.

Johnny is my friend. He later told me what happened the day we met. Johnny had been robbed twice while going down that same street. He was afraid when I walked toward him. He thought I was going to rob him. Then Johnny said, "I heard a Voice behind me. The Voice said, 'It's OK. He's a good guy. He's going to help you.'" God had prompted him, and that's why Johnny let me talk to him that day. Johnny had gotten a revelation, and he chose to believe.

Every choice has a consequence. If you choose to walk off a cliff, you will fall. You wouldn't shake your fist at gravity as you fell. Gravity existed before you chose to step over the edge.

We are given the choice to receive God or reject Him. And like the world we live in, we do not get to determine the consequences of our choices. There are consequences for saying no to God as well. The consequences are revealed in the Bible. God has announced what the choice is. The choice is eternal life or death.

We have the power to choose. Just like Adam, there are two trees before us. Adam had to choose to obey. We must choose to believe. We can choose to enter into a life filled with excitement and hope. We can choose a life where nothing is impossible.

You can choose to have a loving relationship with God that will produce peace and contentment in your heart. You have a say in what happens in your life. You have been given the power of choice. Choose life.

- You will feel freedom and strength rising in your heart.

- You will take that freedom and make correct choices that will produce supernatural results.

- You will choose to believe God for every promise He reveals to you.

- Every good choice you make will propel you forward and higher.

- You will live a life without natural limitations!

6

BULLSEYE

HIT THE TARGET

One day the Lord told me to take my daughter to shoot bow and arrows, so I picked her up at the college campus. We had the indoor shooting range to ourselves. We took turns shooting the arrows into the target. Seeing the arrows fly through the air and hearing them strike the target was fun. It was only forty feet to the target, yet we felt a sense of satisfaction each time an arrow hit its mark.

We had a system: shoot the arrows into the target and then retrieve them. I would hold the target down as my daughter pulled each one of the bright orange arrows out. Then the impossible happened.

On one occasion we had retrieved each of the arrows and returned to our shooting position. Then I shouted, "What is that?!" We both stood there perplexed and amazed. An arrow was in the bullseye of the target!

An arrow had supernaturally appeared as we walked back to shoot again. It was positioned in a spot that would've been directly between us just seconds earlier. God was using this encounter to speak to us. The arrow had been divinely positioned.

When people choose to enter a relationship with God, they begin a life based on faith. A life based on faith means impossible things can happen. Impossible things happen because faith connects them to God and nothing is impossible with Him.

The Cambridge English Dictionary defines "faith" as "*great trust or confidence in something or someone.*"

The reality is that everyone lives by faith or some type of belief system. People are always placing their trust in one thing or another. For instance, many place their faith in their intellect, their money, or their government. They have missed the target.

Some scientists and scholars today scoff at the notion that their lives are based on faith. Yet we have seen scientific theories that have been held out as "true" for many years, only to have those "truths" shaken by new scientific discoveries. By definition, a theory must be falsifiable. This means that a theory must be able to be disproved, otherwise it is a law.

Ultimately, their beliefs were really a type of faith expressed in intellectual terms.

This is not to say that if someone places their trust in God they cannot be intellectual or engage in the pursuit of scientific understanding. Faith in God and the pursuit of scientific truth are not mutually exclusive. As time goes by, science is affirming the worldview as expressed in the Bible. For instance, many publications today present verifiable scientific findings that point to an Intelligent Designer for the explanation of the origins of our universe.

Faith is directional.

Faith is directional. In other words, we choose to direct our trust toward something or someone by an act of our will. You can aim your trust just as you can aim an arrow. When we direct our faith toward God, we open ourselves up to receive all that He can provide, including truth.

Some view faith as a crutch used only by weak or insecure people. But consider the true reality of faith. Suppose this all-powerful God with limitless resources has offered to provide all that is necessary to live a good and fulfilling life. Now suppose that this life is easily and completely accessed by directing faith toward Him. It seems to me that declining God's offer of unlimited help is not being strong but rather being foolish. In reality, to live a life of faith directed toward God is not being weak but being wise.

Would a person really decline the unlimited assistance from an all-powerful God simply because they do not want to appear weak? This reflects a mind that is confused about their position in relation to the God of all creation. A person that walks with this attitude has come to the conclusion that they are the source or may obtain the source of all of their needs. They have become the target of their own faith. Therefore, they have become their own god.

A person with properly directed faith can live a truly remarkable life. Let's consider Moses. God called Moses to go to Egypt and lead His people out of bondage. During their initial meeting, Moses asked God who he should say had sent him. God instructed Moses to tell them *I Am that I Am* sent him.[22] This was God's way of saying that He is the One that eternally exists and is the source of all things. The fact that God is the source of everything makes Him God.

When we believe God for something, we are worshiping Him as the One that can provide the very thing we need. For instance, imagine that you had an injury in your foot, so you direct your faith toward God and ask Him to heal you. You are declaring that God is the source of healing. When you direct your faith toward God, you are worshiping Him as the God that heals. You are elevating Him above your circumstances, above what natural law would say, and even what your own intellect would suggest.

God is elevated in your heart above all other gods.

Faith assigns value to the target of its affections. Faith elevates and exalts the One in whom it is directed. When we direct our faith toward God, we elevate and place value to Him within our hearts. So here is another answer to my question: Faith is the purest form of worship.

Answer #5 - Faith is the purest form of worship.

The idea of faith being the purest form of worship reveals a key to living a life where nothing is impossible. Let's consider Moses again for an example. Moses was a man that had amazing encounters with God and demonstrated unparalleled signs and wonders. He lived a life where truly nothing was impossible.

Moses had an amazing relationship with God.

There is a story in the Bible that reveals a key to his success. This event included Moses' brother and sister, Aaron and Miriam (see Numbers 12:1-8). They confronted Moses because he had married a woman they did not approve of. The two siblings informed Moses that they also had a connection with God.

At this point, God appeared and defended Moses before Aaron and Miriam. God declared that the relationship He had with Moses was special:

Numbers 12:6-8 NKJV

"Hear now My words:

If there is a prophet among you,

I, the LORD, make Myself known to him in a vision;

I speak to him in a dream.

Not so with My servant Moses;

He is faithful in all My house.

I speak with him face to face,

Even plainly, and not in dark sayings;

And he sees the form of the LORD.

Why then were you not afraid

To speak against My servant Moses?"

Moses had something with God that no one else had. Numbers 12:3 says, *"Now the man Moses was very humble, more than all men who were on the face of the earth."* Moses was the most humble man on the earth! That's a bold statement.

The word "humble" in that verse portrays someone with a demeanor of being in need. Moses had placed his faith in God. His faith expressed an attitude that elevated God above himself. This attitude exalted God as the source of all things, the "*I Am*." This walk of humility before God positioned Moses into the place to receive all things. He was properly positioned with God.

Faith declares that God is the source of all good things and positions us to receive all good things from Him. So here is another answer to my question: Faith divinely positions us with God.

Answer #6 - Faith divinely positions us with God.

Our faith came from God. Our faith elevates God in relation to ourselves. Therefore, when we direct faith toward Him, we are divinely positioned to receive. No person can come to God without faith. Jesus said, "*No one can come to Me unless the Father who sent Me draws him*" (John 6:44 NKJV). In writing to the Corinthians, Paul made it clear that everything spiritually good was given to us (see 1 Corinthians

4:7). No person can look at anything they possess and declare, "I got this myself." God remains the source of all good things, including our faith.

God has provided everything. He provided the remedy and the ability to believe for it. All we can do is humble ourselves like Moses and turn to Him with our hearts. God will turn to us and cause our faith to become strong.

Zechariah 1:3 NKJV
Therefore say to them, 'Thus says the LORD of hosts:
"Return to Me," says the LORD of hosts,
"and I will return to you," says the LORD of hosts.

James 4:8 NKJV
Draw near to God and He will draw near to you.

God lifts us up as we humble ourselves before Him. Moses was extremely humble before God; this gave him an extremely high place on the earth. Moses demonstrated power and authority unlike any man since Adam. God entrusted Moses with this amazing authority and power.

At one point God was giving instructions to Moses about dealing with one of the most powerful men on the earth. The Lord said, "*See, I have made you as God to Pharaoh, and Aaron your brother shall be your prophet*" (Exodus 7:1 NKJV). The Pharaoh of Egypt ruled over one of the most powerful nations the earth had ever seen. Yet next to Moses, he was not so big. When we are properly positioned with God, it changes our position in the world and the size of our opposition.

Directing our faith to Jesus expresses continuous pure worship to Him. We are also positioned properly as a result. He grants power and authority to us as we yield to Him. The Bible says that when we trust in Jesus, we are seated with Him in Heavenly places. Jesus is enthroned next to the Father in Heaven and is demonstrating His authority on earth through His people today.

Ephesians 2:4-7 NKJV
But God, who is rich in mercy, because of His great love with which He loved us, even when we were dead in trespasses, made us alive together with Christ (by grace you have been saved), and raised us up together, and made us sit together in the Heavenly places in Christ Jesus, that in the ages to come He might show the exceeding riches of His grace in His kindness toward us in Christ Jesus.

MAE AND THE BRICK

One day we were standing next to a road talking to our friend Lee. The Lord had healed his torn knee ligaments the previous year. He was homeless, so we would stop and visit when we saw him. On this particular day, Lee suddenly looked up with an expression of fear. While gazing at the adjacent field about a hundred yards away, Lee said, "Oh no, she is going to kill my friend Mae!"

A frail woman was staggering across the field. Behind her was a younger woman chasing her and holding up a brick while screaming, "I'm going to kill you, Mae!" This woman seemed totally crazy and determined to murder Mae.

Without much thought and in a low tone I whispered, "In the name of Jesus, I bind you, foul demon... I command you to stop, drop the brick, and turn around."

Instantly the younger woman stopped, dropped the brick, and turned around!

Lee looked at me and said, "Whoa! It worked!"

These two women were at least a hundred yards away. The volume of my voice was just above a whisper when I spoke. There is no way they could have heard me in the natural. No screaming or yelling was necessary. God had demonstrated His authority.

The Bible says that God gives grace to the humble but resists the proud. Grace means God's favor and enabling influence moving upon a person to give them what they need. Remember, God desires to have a relationship. He won't provide grace to people if it would encourage them to be distant from Himself. People that walk in pride before God are out of position to receive His blessings. His blessings are connected to relationship with Him, because that's what He desires. He is a good Dad. Faith requires that we become dependent on Him. Real faith provides pure worship to God and properly positions us.

God has given you a measure of faith. Imagine that you can aim your faith toward God. You are now divinely positioned to receive all that God longs to give you. You are properly positioned to see His provision strike the ground that you occupy. You are correctly positioned to have your dreams fulfilled. He becomes your Father and you get all the benefits of being His child.

- You direct your faith toward God.

- Your faith expresses pure worship to Him.

- You are divinely positioned with Him.

- You have intimate communion with Him.

- You receive all that He has to offer.

- Nothing is impossible!

7

LOOK HOW BEAUTIFUL 7-ELEVEN IS!

MARIO AND THE 7-ELEVEN

One day we saw a man limping along a major street. You could tell that he was in pain. Imagine someone walking barefoot over broken glass. That's what he looked like. We asked if we could pray for him. He said that his name was Mario and that his feet were covered with painful sores. He could not even wear socks due to the pain. We asked Jesus to heal him and remove the pain. Mario looked up with an expression of shock and said, "There is no pain!" He walked around shaking his head in amazement.

I sensed the Lord wanted us to pray for Mario's eyes. I asked if he could see very well. He said, "I don't see very good close up or faraway." So then we touched his eyes and asked Jesus to heal him. Mario opened his eyes and exclaimed, "Look how beautiful the 7-Eleven store is!" We tried to see if his eyesight was better, but Mario seemed distracted as he excitedly looked around. He looked down at the grass and said, "Is that what it looks like? Look how beautiful it is!" He looked up at the sky like a child seeing it for the first time.

It took a moment for us realize that Mario was seeing color for the first time! The vibrant greens of the grass and the brilliant blue of the sky were all new to him. Mario told us that before we prayed he could only see in shades of gray. Not only did God heal his color blindness, but now he was able to read letters on a sign several blocks away and the small words of the Bible app on my phone. Jesus had healed his vision and removed his color blindness!

Mario was seeing the whole world in a brand-new way. Faith allows people to see things the way God intended.

Have you ever heard the expression, "Seeing with the eyes of your heart"? I once heard an illustration given by a minister named William Branham. Imagine that you see me now standing next to one of my sons. Suppose now that he is blindfolded. As I am speaking, he instantly knows that his father is standing next to him. He cannot see me with his eyes. He only knows that his father is standing next to him because of his sense of hearing. And yet with only one natural sense he knows beyond any doubt that I'm standing there. He cannot feel, see, smell, or taste the fact that I am next to him. And yet he is so certain that it is his father standing there that he would be willing to bet everything. With his sense of hearing he is able to see me in his mind's eye. He knows what I look like and where I'm standing. His confidence is unshakable even though it is based entirely on only one of his five senses.

This is what faith is like. Faith allows us to see with the eyes of our heart. We don't need any other sense to give us confidence in something that our faith sees.

Faith is like a sixth sense. Faith is different from our natural senses because it's spiritual. With this single spiritual sense we can know something with such confidence that we would be willing to bet our life on it.

Here is another answer to my question: Faith sees the world as it should be.

Answer #7 - Faith sees the world as it should be.

Faith sees our world as it should be according to God. Paul stated that Moses was led by what he saw with his faith and not by what he saw with his natural senses.

Hebrews 11:27 NKJV
By faith he forsook Egypt, not fearing the wrath of the king; for he endured as seeing Him who is invisible.

The Bible says we are to walk by faith and not by sight. Moses did incredible things because he was led by what he could see with his faith. What Moses saw with his faith overpowered everything in the natural. This is how faith becomes effective. We allow our faith to direct us regardless of what we are sensing in the natural world.

We shape our natural world from the unseen world when we are led by our faith. We are designed to live in a way that our existence is changed from the eternal realm. When we are led by our faith, we are living from a place where there are no impossibilities.

Everything we can see in our world originated from the eternal realm. Imagine an invisible veil separating the natural world and the eternal realm. Existence on the other side of the veil is more real and permanent than in the natural world. Everything we see in the natural came from the other side of the veil. The eternal realm contains everything needed to affect change in this world.

Hebrews 11:3 NKJV
By faith we understand that the worlds were framed by the word of God, so that the things which are seen were not made of things which are visible.

Faith is like a bridge between the eternal realm and the natural world. Faith gives us access to God who is the source of everything. Faith also gives us access to God's promises. Many of God's promises were intended to be manifested in this world. God promised healing, protection, provision, and many other things. These things won't be needed in eternity.

Faith is the substance of the things that we hope for and the evidence that it exists. The stuff on the other side of the veil can be seen by our faith. God will release a revelation of something He desires to give us. Once we see it, then we know we can have it. Remember that God is a rewarder of those who seek Him. It's through this process that God has chosen to rule the natural world from the eternal realm.

God used the same system in the garden with Adam. He created all of the animals, then caused them to pass in front of Adam.

Genesis 2:19 NKJV
Out of the ground the LORD God formed every beast of the field and every bird of the air, and brought them to Adam to see what he would call them. And whatever Adam called each living creature, that was its name.

The Bible says God did this to see what Adam would name each animal. God revealed to Adam that he could do this. The original language for the word "name" is better translated as honor, authority, or character. I believe that when Adam "named" each animal, he was assigning characteristics and traits to them. In any event, Adam was synchronized with his Father and co-labored with Him.

Jesus, the second Adam, also co-labored with His Father. Jesus said He didn't do anything without His Father. Jesus only did what He saw the Father do. The Father showed the works to Jesus, then Jesus did the works. Jesus and the Father were in perfect unity.

John 5:19-20 NKJV
Then Jesus answered and said to them, "Most assuredly, I say to you, the Son can do nothing of Himself, but what He sees the Father do; for whatever He does, the Son also does in like manner. For the Father loves the Son, and shows Him all things that He Himself does; and He will

show Him greater works than these,
that you may marvel.

Jesus said that we cannot do anything without Him.
Jesus also said that He sends His followers into the
world, just as the Father sent Him. We do the works
through Jesus, just as Jesus did the works through the
Father. This is the result of relationship. We are to be
in unity with Jesus as He is one with the Father. This
results in our doing what He is doing.

John 15:5 NKJV
"I am the vine, you are the branches. He who abides in
Me, and I in him, bears much fruit; for without Me you
can do nothing.

John 20:21 NKJV
So Jesus said to them again, "Peace to you!
As the Father has sent Me, I also send you."

We are made up of a spirit, soul, and body. The soul
and body constitute what the Bible calls our flesh. We
are never to be led by our flesh because it wants to be
ruled by the natural world.

The soul includes our mind, will, and emotions.
Many people are limited by what they can intellectually understand. It doesn't matter how brilliant the
person is; they are infinitely short of what is avail-

able. This means that they are limited by what they can understand. They have excluded the part within themselves that can access the impossible.

It's as if they have declared, "I refuse to worship God until I can contain Him within my mind." This would be a relatively very small god and hardly worth worshiping. And yet many today worship their own intellects above the God who created them.

Some people have been mastered by their emotions. Many have been enslaved by fear. When we cling to our feelings, they begin to have control over us like a cruel taskmaster. This cruel master refuses to allow access to God's promises or the impossible.

And there are people who have come to believe they are only a higher evolved animal. They have chosen to live a life where the only goal is to satisfy the impulses and cravings of their flesh. They too have been enslaved by a part of their being that was never intended to rule over them.

Our minds, emotions, and bodies were given to us from God. They are amazing and wonderful. However, God did not intend for them to lead us. We are created to be led by God through our spirits. This is the realm of faith. William Branham once said, "Our minds are of the flesh and faith is of God… and

God is always correct."

GIVE ME A HAND

My brother, a local pastor, and I had made a quick trip to the store to get refreshments for the family. We were standing in line waiting to check out when I saw a young man ahead of us. He was wearing a brace on his hand, and I knew the Lord wanted us to pray for him.

By faith we can see the world as God wants it to be.

My brother checked out as I followed the young man with the brace outside. He said his name was Jason and that he had injured his hand. Jason said, "I broke my hand trying to drive it through a windshield." His pain level was very high, and a bone bulged out of the back of his hand.

I said, "Let's pray and ask Jesus to heal it." The three of us prayed asking Jesus to heal Jason's hand.

Jason said, "I can feel tingling in my hand." He took the brace off and started to flex his wrist and hand.

I asked, "How's the pain?"

He said, "There is no pain!"

I asked, "Where is the bulging bone?"

Jason said, "It's gone!"

Jason had received a fresh revelation of how much Jesus loved him. He shook our hands good-bye with a firm squeeze!

Faith is the currency of Heaven because God does not want us to be led by our flesh—minds, emotions, and bodies. He intends for us to be led by the Spirit. It is by faith that He accomplishes this, because faith is of the Spirit.

By faith we can see our world as God wants it to be. Faith allows you to co-labor with God in creating your world. Faith is a higher, nobler way to live. Faith is the principal thing.

What do you see? People perish for lack of vision. Can you see God's plan for your life? Can you see God's plan for our world? Remember that God deeply desires to have a relationship with you. He will open the eyes of your heart and give you a vision for your life when you turn to Him. You will receive what He reveals as you keep your faith directed to Him.

Proverbs 29:18 MSG
If people can't see what God is doing,
they stumble all over themselves;
But when they attend to what he reveals,
they are most blessed.

- You turn to God in faith.

- You are led by the Spirit.

- The eyes of your
  heart are open.

- You can see with your faith.

- God is giving you a
  vision for your life.

- You co-labor with God.

- You live a life that
  is most blessed!

8

TAKE IT EASY

THE HOUSE CALL

We were taking it easy. A typical evening at home enjoying a movie and pizza. Kallie, my daughter's friend, was getting up from the couch when she cringed and said, "Ouch, my shoulder!" She had torn her rotator cuff playing softball in high school and couldn't raise her arm above her shoulder without pain.

I asked, "Would you like for it to be healed?"

She jokingly said, "Sure, why, do you have a scalpel?"

I said, "No, but I think Jesus will heal you."

We asked Kallie to sit in a chair in the middle of our living room. Then we gathered around and asked Jesus to heal her. She immediately began to shake and cry. I asked, "What's going on?"

She said, "I can feel Him! It feels like a hand inside my shoulder!"

After a couple of minutes I said, "Try it out. Raise your arm." She shook her head no. I said, "Go ahead, try it out."

Kallie slowly raised her arm until it was straight up. She said, "No pain!" She was totally healed. Jesus had made a house call!

The early church was small in numbers and did not have many of the natural resources available to Christians today. And yet they were able to impact the entire world.

Though few in numbers, they were able to accomplish amazing results. The message of God's love and salvation spread quickly. Miracles, signs, and wonders were routinely performed. These men and women did great things through faith.

The Apostle Paul said that anything done apart from faith—in other words, sin—is contrary to God.[23] How can we become effective like the early church? We must learn how to take it easy. We can go back to the very beginning of creation to see the significance of taking it easy.

Some people get tripped up when it comes to discussing Biblical creation. They intellectually struggle because, according to the Bible, everything was created in six days. The struggle occurs in people's intellects.

Science has not caught up with the Bible. Many of the truths expressed in the Bible do not line up with man's current understanding of natural law. The truths in the Bible are not bound by natural law. God established natural law and is therefore not bound to it.

Man's understanding of time itself is changing. Scientists now know that time is not static but can speed up or slow down. For instance, time can be affected by gravity and speed.

Albert Einstein once taught that the universe is static. Science has since discovered that our universe is expanding and that the expansion is accelerating. The Bible declared this a long time ago. In fact, the Bible revealed that the earth was round long before men knew it to be true.

Isaiah 40:22 NKJV
It is He who sits above the circle of the earth,
And its inhabitants are like grasshoppers,
Who stretches out the heavens like a curtain,
And spreads them out like a tent to dwell in.

The Bible has always been ahead of man's understanding of truth because the Bible points to the One who is the source of all truth. Seeing with the eyes of our heart—our faith—can help us to understand things currently beyond our intellect.

We see in the book of Genesis, God created everything in six days and then rested on the seventh day. It was finished. There was no sin, decay, or death. Adam and Eve lived in a paradise on earth and in perfect fellowship with God. God declared that the seventh day was sacred because He had completed creation and then rested.

The Bible gives an account of when God spoke to the children of Israel near Mount Sinai. God brought up the seventh day again when He gave them the Ten Commandments. He called it the Sabbath day and told them to honor it by not working.[24]

The term "Sabbath" means "intermission." The original Hebrew word came from a word that means "desist from exertion." Honoring the Sabbath was a way to worship and remember God as Creator.

The Apostle Paul understood what the Sabbath pointed to. He wrote about it in the book of Hebrews, Chapters 3 and 4 of the Bible. Paul used the story of the children of Israel during their time in the desert. God had led them out of the bondage of Egypt and into the desert. He had desired to take them into the Promised Land. It was to be a place where darkness would be subdued. It was to be a land flowing with milk and honey for anyone that would come to Him. It was to be the land of rest. The Sabbath pointed to God's plan for the restoration of His original design intent.

Paul said that the people failed to enter into the land of rest because of their unbelief. They had heard God's promises to live a blessed life there. However, God's word did not help them because they did not believe. So God declared that they would not enter into His rest because of their unbelief.[25]

According to the Apostle Paul, we enter into God's rest when we believe in Jesus. This is not a future rest in Heaven but a relationship here in this life. Paul wrote, "*For we who have believed do enter that rest*" (Hebrews 4:3 NKJV).

Entering into God's rest is accomplished by believing in Jesus. But what does it mean to enter God's rest? Paul wrote, "*For he who has entered His rest has himself also ceased from his works as God did from His*" (Hebrews 4:10 NKJV). Entering into God's rest means that we have ceased from our own works as

God rested after He finished creating everything.[26] That's what the Sabbath pointed to.

We believe in Jesus, and He gives us rest. His rest means that we cease from our own works. We stop striving to be good, to please God, and to overcome evil by our own works. Jesus has done all of these things for us. The work is finished. Jesus cried out from the cross, "*It is finished!*"[27] Our part is to believe. Believing will bring forth God's works.

Rest means that God's works are manifesting through us to accomplish everything. Jesus has made us pleasing to God, He makes us good, He overcomes evil. Jesus has completed everything necessary to bring forth God's new creations. We are God's new creations being brought forth on the earth.

We are God's new creations being brought forth on the earth.

We enter into His rest and then cease from our own works. This does not mean we stop being active or stop doing things for God. This means that whatever things we do are His works coming through us. Faith leads us into God's rest which manifests His life through us.

Psalms, Chapter 90 was written by Moses. He knew there was a better way and prayed for it. Moses expressed his desire in verses 16 and 17: "*Let Your work appear to Your servants, And Your glory to their children. And let the beauty of the LORD our God be upon us, And establish the work of our hands for us; Yes, establish the work of our hands.*" Moses longed to see God manifest His works through all of His people.

Real faith properly directed toward God will lead people into the rest of God. This means that we stop striving to please God with our own abilities. Jesus declared, "*Come to Me, all you who labor and are heavy laden, and I will give you rest.*" He went on to say, "*For My yoke is easy and My burden is light.*" I like the Message version of these verses found in Matthew 11:28-30:

Matthew 11:28-30 MSG

"Are you tired? Worn out? Burned out on religion? Come to me. Get away with me and you'll recover your life. I'll show you how to take a real rest. Walk with me and work with me—watch how I do it. Learn the unforced rhythms of grace. I won't lay anything heavy or ill-fitting on you. Keep company with me and you'll learn to live freely and lightly."

Faith leads us into God's "rest." This "rest" places the focus on what God has done, is doing, and will do on our behalf. The emphasis is on Him and His abilities, not ours. Faith requires a posture of "rest" in our hearts to access the impossible. Everyone must come to the end of themselves. There are limitless possibilities beyond that point.

It's not really about your being diminished; it's about the real you coming forth, which is His original design for us. It's not that God doesn't like us, but He wants the "real" us to come forward. We are supposed to die to ourselves, but it's more like a caterpillar dying to itself and the "real" creature manifesting—which is a beautiful butterfly.[28] That's the real creature. That's what God wants for us. The butterfly comes forth after the caterpillar enters into a state of rest while hanging from a tree branch.

This leads us to yet another answer to my question as to why God made faith the currency of Heaven: Faith provides rest.

Answer #8 - Faith provides rest.

Jesus supernaturally fed more than five-thousand people with only five loaves of bread and two fish (see John 6:5-14). He simply prayed, then His disciples handed out the food. Everyone got to eat, and there was plenty left over. The Bible says there was a lot of grass where this occurred. It's interesting that before feeding everyone, Jesus instructed His disciples, "*Make the people sit down.*"

That miracle only happened after everyone assumed a posture of rest on the green grass and in the Presence of the Shepherd. Miracles happen when we have a posture of rest in our hearts while in His Presence. We direct our faith toward His abilities and away from our own. Then we are ready to be miraculously fed by Him. Centuries before this event, King David wrote in Psalm 23:

Psalms 23:1-3 NKJV
A Psalm of David.
The Lᴏʀᴅ is my shepherd;
I shall not want.
He makes me to lie down in green pastures;
He leads me beside the still waters.
He restores my soul;
He leads me in the paths of righteousness
For His name's sake.

Psalm 23 says that the Lord leads us beside still waters. After that miraculous meal, Jesus went to the other side of a lake near a town. A crowd of people soon gathered around Jesus and asked Him a very good question: "*[W]hat shall we do, that we may work the works of God?"* Jesus very clearly answered their question! He said, *"[T]his is the work of God, that you believe in Him whom He sent"* (see John 6:28-29). That's it! How are we to work the works of God? You might say that our job description can be summed up in one sentence. Believe in Jesus.

Imagine Jesus saying:

I love you, believe Me,

I will be in you,

I will give you a new heart,

You will do what I did,

I will never leave you,

I will give to you whatever you ask,

When I say, nothing is impossible,

... believe Me.

CAN YOU HEAR?

A family friend named Billie asked Kristen and I to come over to pray for a three-year-old relative of hers named Ozcar. The doctor said Ozcar was deaf. According to Billie, Ozcar could not really talk but could only say one or two words.

Ozcar was asleep when we arrived. The three of us stood next to the bed talking. We were speaking in a normal manner, and yet he never moved. He clearly could not hear us.

We asked Jesus to heal him and commanded deafness to leave. I lightly placed a finger in each ear as we prayed. We could feel a distinct heat around Ozcar's head.

Ozcar began to wake up. I whistled softly while standing off to his left. He slowly raised his hand to touch his left ear. Ozcar's eyes then quickly shot open as he turned his head to look. Ozcar was hearing! Jesus healed him completely!

We spent the next hour watching him play. Ozcar was hearing the smallest sounds. At one point, he suddenly stopped and told us, "Shuuuush (be quiet)!" He made a gesture with his hand as though he was trying to hear something outside. We paused and got quiet… and we could hear the faint sound of kids playing down the street. He now had excellent hearing!

The family took Ozcar back to the doctor. After re-examining him the doctor said Ozcar's hearing was fine!

Jesus instructed His followers to heal sick people, raise people from the dead, and cast out demons.[29] They were to declare that the Kingdom of God was at hand. Jesus gave other instructions before departing the earth. His followers were to be active. It was understood that He would produce the works through them. It's clear that God's rest would not result in a lack of activity.

We also know that this activity would seem easy and light because He said, "*For My yoke is easy and My burden is light*" (Matthew 11:30 NKJV). These activities were to be the works of God manifesting through His people, accomplished by faith and from a posture of rest. They were to do mighty miracles, signs, and wonders. They were to do these incredible things and yet not strive under their own resources.

Real faith requires that we live in a continual Sabbath rest. This rest is not optional if we are going to have a mature faith.

Some Christians daydream about what it must have been like to walk with Jesus as the disciples did. The original disciples had spent three years following and living with Jesus. They had seen Him turn water into wine, heal the sick, and raise the dead. They had never known such peace and purpose before. Then Jesus gave them the news of His coming departure. Imagine the scene: Jesus said He was going to be killed and was going away. Dread and fear filled the disciples' hearts.

Then Jesus said something really amazing: "*It is to your advantage that I go away*" (John 16:7 NKJV). Don't quickly pass by that comment; Jesus said His leaving did not mean there would be a drop-off or letdown. He said things would be better for them. He said they would do what He did and even greater things because He was going to send His Presence, the Holy Spirit, to them.

According to the Bible, the indwelling of the Holy Spirit is supposed to be just like having Jesus right there with the person (2 Corinthians 3:17). Jesus is not only with His disciples, but now He is in them. His Presence is in His people today, and He is producing works through them. God is restoring things to His original-design intent. We are to live in the seventh day, a continual Sabbath rest, where His works are finished. This is the "rest" of God.

God's rest is always connected to His Presence. Faith gives us access to Him, and this is what produces His works in our lives.

John 16:5-7 NKJV
But now I go away to Him who sent Me, and none of you asks Me, 'Where are You going?' But because I have said these things to you, sorrow has filled your heart.

> Nevertheless I tell you the truth. It is to your advantage
> that I go away; for if I do not go away, the Helper will not
> come to you; but if I depart, I will send Him to you.

Without His Presence in our life, we will strive under our own efforts. Striving under our own efforts will never produce anything of eternal value. It's critical that we have God's Presence working in our lives.

Real faith properly directed to God will guide you into a place where striving has ceased. All the resources of Heaven vanquish the presence of evil in this place. This is a place of peace and contentment. This is a place flowing with milk and honey.

You will change your world when you enter into God's rest and live from His manifested Presence. It will be easy and light.

Stop trying to make God love you. Stop trying to please Him. Rest says, "God loves you and there is nothing you can do to change that!" Take it easy and believe!

Galatians 3:5 MSG
Answer this question: Does the God who lavishly provides you with his own presence, his Holy Spirit, working things in your lives you could never do for yourselves, does he do these things because of your strenuous moral striving or because you trust him to do them in you?

- You have stopped striving under your own energy.

- You embrace God's Presence.

- Your life with God is easy and light.

- The unlimited power of God is working in you.

- Nothing is impossible for you!

9

WHAT'S THE PLAN

THE BAPTIST AND THE WARLOCK

One day I was driving near my office when I saw a young woman walking with crutches. She was in pain and crying. Amie had a minor legal problem and needed to come up with some money by the end of the day, or a warrant was going to be issued for her arrest. Her brother, Bryan, had walked several blocks ahead of her to the blood plasma center. They were going to donate blood for money. However, with the broken bone in her foot she could only hobble behind.

I asked about her faith. She said, "I believe in Jesus, I'm Baptist." Kneeling down and putting my hand on her foot, I asked Jesus to heal her. Amie was startled as her foot popped! She said, "The pain is gone!" She walked around crying and holding up the crutches.

The Lord told me to get the money she needed, so we agreed to meet at the blood plasma center. She said,

"Bryan needs prayer too, but he doesn't like God."

I said, "We will pray, and then he will like God."

I soon arrived with the money. Her brother was glaring at me as I got out of my car. I walked up and handed Amie the money. She tried to refuse it, but I said, "The Lord told me to give it to you, 'for free.'" So, with tears, she accepted it.

I turned to Bryan and asked, "What do you need?" He said he had a torn rotator cuff which popped and caused pain. I put my hand on his shoulder and asked Jesus to heal him. Then I said, "Try it out. Raise your arm." He raised his arm and instantly looked at Amie with an expression of shock.

Amie said, "Right? I know!" There was no pain or popping!

Bryan said, "I don't understand why God would heal me."

I said, "Because He loves you."

Bryan said, "You don't understand. I'm a warlock. I practice witchcraft."

I then said, "You have been tapping into evil forces for power. You have to do things for them before they give you power. Someday they will collect, and it will cost you everything. Jesus just healed you 'for free.' He healed you because He loves you. He has paid for you.

You must choose to accept Him. Nothing is close to God's power."

The Lord then revealed some things to me about Bryan. I said, "You have felt different since you were a little boy. You could see things that others couldn't. You have gifts that were given to you by God, but the enemy has tricked you into serving them."

Bryan said, "Yes, I could see your aura when you got out of your car. It was like ten feet tall! I knew there was something different about you."

I said, "That wasn't my aura, that was the anointing of God."

Jesus demonstrated His love in front of the blood plasma center. He had already given His blood for them.

Amie went away filled with joy and a stronger faith. Bryan left with the revelation that God loved him. He went away with the choice directly before him. I don't know what happened to Bryan, but I know that God always finishes what He starts.

The Bible talks about the anointing of God. What is meant by the term "*anointing*"? I once heard my minister friend Bobby Conner say, "The anointing is the Presence of God, with power, for purpose." The

Holy Spirit is working in the world today through God's people. God is manifesting His Presence and demonstrating His power in order to restore faith.

Acts 10:38 NKJV
how God anointed Jesus of Nazareth with the Holy Spirit and with power, who went about doing good and healing all who were oppressed by the devil, for God was with Him.

And why is that a big deal? The Apostle John wrote, "*For whatever is born of God overcomes the world. And this is the victory that has overcome the world—our faith*" (1 John 5:4 NKJV).

What overcomes the world? Your faith. What did John mean by "*the world*"? It means the world system. The Bible talks about "the prince of the power of the air" in the world today—the devil.[30]

Adam handed his authority to the devil when he chose to believe the devil's lie and to disbelieve God. This is the reason for everything bad in the world. The list of things caused by the devil's influence includes death, sickness, poverty, murder, racism, and on and on.

Let's revisit the story of Adam and Eve in the garden near Eden.

They were created beings. God said, "*Let Us make*

man in our image." Together Adam and Eve reflected God's image. They were not an exact copy of God but a resemblance of Him. God's original desire was that all mankind would reflect Him.

God gave Adam dominion over every created thing—everything that crawled, walked, swam, and flew. Adam even had dominion over spiritual creatures. Dominion means authority to rule.

Imagine that Adam could call to a tiger, "Come here and sit." The tiger would immediately come running and sit. Maybe Adam could then bless the tiger and pat him on the head before sending him away. There was nothing alive or created that Adam and Eve did not have authority over.

God said He wanted them to multiply and subdue the earth. They had an assignment. They were to have a relationship with God, reflect His image, rule over the earth, and have children like themselves.

At this time the devil was on the earth, and he was mad. Previously the devil was the highest-level angel in Heaven. But one day he decided he wanted to be God. So he gathered up many angels and convinced them to join in on a rebellion against God. Even the angels in Heaven were created with the ability to choose.

God then cast the devil and the other rebellious angels out of Heaven. God removed His glory from them, and now they are called demons. That's what the devil is: a created being thrown out of Heaven. He is not anywhere close to Jesus. Jesus was not created. Jesus is the Creator.

Imagine the scene in the beginning. The devil and his gang had been cast out of Heaven. They had to live with the knowledge that this small creature called man had authority over them. The devil hated Adam and Eve because they had dominion and they reflected God's image.

Now the devil must have been very motivated to do something about this. He must have thought long and hard about how he could remove them. I'm certain that the devil would have killed them immediately if he could. But what could he do? He realized that there was one weapon in his arsenal that may work—the lie.

The devil whispered lies into the ears of these humans created in God's image. He could not kill them. He used the only weapon available that would work. It was the lie.

The devil started with Eve. "Did God really say? Did God really say if you eat from the forbidden tree that you would die?" That was the seed. That was the lie the devil uttered.

That was the moment Adam and Eve's defeat occurred. Their defeat was set before they actually ate the forbidden fruit. It happened the moment they chose to entertain the lie. By choice they began to think upon the lie which resulted in believing the devil. Considering the lie eventually led to the act. The lie produced death and decay into the earth.

The devil's plan seemed to work. I can imagine the scene—the devil saying, "Now I am in charge! See, I have the keys to death now. Just think, all I had to do was use the lie!"

The dark forces shouted, "Now we control the world!" They must have been strutting around in a great celebration.

This is what John meant when he said, "*the world.*" He meant this world which is currently overshadowed by the powers of darkness. And what overcomes all of that? Your faith! Your faith is the very thing that can wipe out the devil's plan. The lie brought it in, and the truth overcomes it! Faith is the principal thing.

After Adam and Eve's failure, God immediately began to put a plan into action to restore things to His original intent. God put His plan into motion to take authority away from the devil. In Genesis, Chapter 3, God announced His judgment over the devil for deceiving Adam. God declared that the offspring of Eve would crush his head, which symbolized the destruction of the devil and all of his works.

Genesis 3:15 NKJV
And I will put enmity
Between you and the woman,
And between your seed and her Seed;
He shall bruise your head,
And you shall bruise His heel."

Jesus came into the earth from Heaven and was born from a virgin woman. Jesus is the Son of God, but when He walked among us on earth He referred to Himself as "*Son of Man*." Even though He is God, He lived His life completely as a Man and yet without sin. Therefore, He was the only Man qualified for and capable of completely crushing the devil's head.

In essence, God made certain that His Word would stand. It would be Man that would have dominion over the earth and would reflect God's image.

Jesus said that He came to make us His brothers and His Father our Father (see John 20:17). God is currently restoring things to His original plan. He is doing that through His people.

Romans 8:29 NKJV
For whom He foreknew, He also predestined to be
conformed to the image of His Son, that He might
be the firstborn among many brethren.

Jesus has wiped out the devil's works. Jesus now has the keys to death and hell. Jesus lives in you after you are born again through faith. You now have authority over the devil (see Luke 10:19-20). The enemy is really powerless against you when you are in Jesus. There is only one weapon that will work against you, the same weapon that originally brought Adam down—the lie. Faith is the principal thing.

Jesus, Peter, and Paul all referred to a particular chapter in the Bible. This must be a very important part of the Bible if they referred to it. Take a look at the first four verses of Psalms 110:

Psalms 110:1-4 NKJV
A Psalm of David.
The Lord said to my Lord,
"Sit at My right hand,
Till I make Your enemies Your footstool."
The Lord shall send the rod of Your strength out of Zion.
Rule in the midst of Your enemies!
Your people shall be volunteers

In the day of Your power;
In the beauties of holiness, from the womb of the morning,
You have the dew of Your youth.
The LORD has sworn
And will not relent,
"You are a priest forever
According to the order of Melchizedek."

What does it mean? It's a glimpse of Father God talking to God the Son. It's as if the Father looks to His right and says, "Jesus, take a seat until We destroy all of the work done by the devil." Jesus is seated next to the Father until all of their enemies are destroyed. That word "Till" in verse 1 is very important. Jesus is seated next to the Father until His enemies have been made His footstool.

Who are His enemies? The devil, demons, and all of the results of their work. Some of God's enemies include: poverty, racism, sickness, fear, and all sin. In effect, everything that came into the world as a result of Adam's failure is opposed to God. God is defeating all of these things today. He is ruling in the midst of His enemies while seated on His throne. He is doing this by the Person of the Holy Spirit. God's people are volunteering in the day of His power.

Jesus is personally coming back to the earth again.

And yet He has already begun to defeat His enemies from Heaven while being seated next to the Father. He is ruling in the midst of His enemies by working through His people today on earth. He is the Head, and we are the body (see Colossians 1:18).

Hebrews 10:11-14 NKJV
And every priest stands ministering daily and offering repeatedly the same sacrifices, which can never take away sins. But this Man, after He had offered one sacrifice for sins forever, sat down at the right hand of God, from that time waiting till His enemies are made His footstool. For by one offering He has perfected forever those who are being sanctified.

Jesus said that we are occupiers in a foreign land (see Luke 19:13). We are to be about our Father's business just as Jesus was while walking on the earth before going to the cross (see Luke 2:49). We are to be advancing our Father's Kingdom on the earth.

Psalms 115:16 NKJV
The heaven, even the heavens, are the LORD's;
But the earth He has given to the children of men.

He is King and is delegating His authority to us so that we can represent Him here on earth. He has given to us His name, His Word, His Presence, and the assistance of Holy angels so that we can fulfill our assignment.

Many Christians today are paralyzed and waiting for Jesus to come back because things are so bad on the earth. However, God wants to accomplish things through us right now.

We are planted here on earth where darkness still has influence. And so what overcomes all of that? Our faith! It's that simple.

Some say, "It's too simple; it will never work." And yet it does work. The truth is, the battle between God's kingdom and the powers of darkness is not even close. We are not really striving or struggling in this conflict. The demonic power compared to the power of God is not close.

God's plan is to destroy all of the works of the devil. It's your faith that will accomplish His plan. Faith is the principal thing.

WHY DID GOD MAKE FAITH THE CURRENCY OF HEAVEN?

Faith places children at the front of the line.

You can be free to have joy and hope again.

Faith declares that every person is precious to God.

You are highly valued by God.

Faith requires a relationship with God.

You are personally invited to have a relationship with God.

Faith requires a choice.

You have been given the power of choice.

Faith is the purest form of worship.

You have Divine purpose.

Faith divinely positions us with God.

You have been invited to take a seat with Him.

Faith sees the world as it should be.

You can change your world.

Faith provides rest.

You can take it easy.

God has destroyed your enemies.

If you haven't connected to God through Jesus, don't let this moment go by without turning to Him right now. Pray the following prayer:

Dear Jesus,

I believe You are the Son of God. I realize that I have not lived up to Your standards of what is good. I want to be pardoned for everything bad that I have ever done. I believe that Your blood was shed for me. I believe You died for my sins on the cross and then arose from the dead three days later. Please forgive me now. Please come into my heart and become my Savior and King. Please fill me with Your Holy Spirit and make me into all that You desire me to be.

Amen!

Congratulations, you are now born again! That's it! Believing gets the job done. You are now on a path that leads to peace and purpose for your life. Find other people that follow Jesus and hang out with them. Get a Bible and start reading it regularly so you can learn about all the amazing things your new life will bring. The Holy Spirit will guide you and teach you. God is always with you!

10

DO YOU WANT MORE?

So how can we increase our faith? How do we develop a faith that can obtain God's promises and see the impossible? The Apostle Paul wrote a letter to the Christians in Corinth to correct and encourage them.

Paul reminded them of the basic truth regarding their faith by saying, "*But I fear, lest somehow, as the serpent deceived Eve by his craftiness, so your minds may be corrupted from the simplicity that is in Christ*" (2 Corinthians 11:3).

What we really need is a simple devotion to Jesus. Everything else springs from this essential truth. The enemy is always trying to make God's message confusing and complicated. The devil used the same trick on Eve in the beginning.

2 Corinthians 11:1-3 NKJV
Oh, that you would bear with me in a little folly—
and indeed you do bear with me. For I am jealous for
you with godly jealousy. For I have betrothed you to one

husband, that I may present you as a chaste virgin to
Christ. But I fear, lest somehow, as the serpent deceived
Eve by his craftiness, so your minds may be corrupted
from the simplicity that is in Christ.

LEARN TO BECOME CHILDLIKE
— *Faith places children at the front of the line.*

Learn to trust God without needing to intellectually understand everything in advance. Trust that He
will bring the understanding later. First believe, and
then you will see. Picture God leaning forward with
a desire to bless you. He is the perfect Father you always wanted. See Him as the One who loves, protects,
and cares for you.

Hebrews 11:6 MSG
It's impossible to please God apart from faith. And why?
Because anyone who wants to approach God must
believe both that he exists and that he cares
enough to respond to those who seek him.

VIEW YOURSELF CORRECTLY
— *Faith declares that every single person is precious to God.*

God saw you long before you were born. You are
individually precious to Him. He had wonderful in-
tentions for you from the very beginning. He intends
for you to walk out special and unique assignments

(Psalms 139:14-18). He has plans for you that are only yours, and they are good (Jeremiah 29:11). It's never too late or too early to follow Him. He knows everything about you and loves you completely, unconditionally, and forever. You are precious to God. Jesus said:

Matthew 18:11-13 NKJV
For the Son of Man has come to save that which was lost. "What do you think? If a man has a hundred sheep, and one of them goes astray, does he not leave the ninety-nine and go to the mountains to seek the one that is straying? And if he should find it, assuredly, I say to you, he rejoices more over that sheep than over the ninety-nine that did not go astray.

DRAW NEAR TO GOD
— *Faith requires a relationship.*

Spend time talking to God and listening to Him. Take time to be alone with Him every day. Make yourself become quiet and direct your heart towards Him.

Spend time reading the Bible. The Bible contains truths that have been given to us from God. Reading the Bible will build your faith because God will cause His Word to come alive in your heart.

Turn to God with an open and honest attitude.

Allow Him to reveal things in your life that harm your faith. See Him illuminating areas in your life that He wants to change. Receive these promptings as loving correction and not as condemnation (see Romans 8:1). Quickly agree and ask Him to forgive you and to remove it from your life. Relax and view this as a long term relationship based on His love for you and not your abilities.

1 John 1:8-9 MSG
If we claim that we're free of sin, we're only fooling ourselves. A claim like that is errant nonsense. On the other hand, if we admit our sins—make a clean breast of them—he won't let us down; he'll be true to himself. He'll forgive our sins and purge us of all wrongdoing.

Be honest about the condition of your faith. Let's revisit the story in Mark Chapter 9 where the father brought his son to Jesus to be healed because the disciples couldn't help. Jesus told the father that with proper believing anything was possible. At that moment the father became honest about his faith.

Mark 9:23-24 NKJV
Jesus said to him, "If you can believe, all things are possible to him who believes." Immediately the father of the child cried out and said with tears, "Lord, I believe; help my unbelief!"

The father of the child told Jesus that he only had enough faith to ask for help. In essence, the father was asking Jesus to help with his unbelief. Jesus responded to this honesty by immediately healing the man's son. The Lord helped the man's unbelief by demonstrating His love and compassion.

I'm certain that the father and his son left that day with greater faith. Being honest about the condition of our faith is key to growing in faith. God is the source of your faith, and He is the only One who can increase it.

USE YOUR POWER TO CHOOSE

— *Faith requires choice.*

Come into agreement with what God has said about you. Read the Bible and allow the Holy Spirit to guide and teach you. Ask God to bring a revelation of how much real power you have in Him. See every dark confrontation and inner struggle as opportunities to exercise your power to choose life. Make the choice to call upon God for help. He longs to give you what you need.

The devil is terrified of the day when you discover that you have the power to choose. Learning to choose is connected to our learning to walk in dominion over evil.

Choose to eat from the *Tree of Life* each day by spending time with Jesus. Choose to reject what the world and the enemy says about you. Choose to believe what God has said and expect Him to back it up with all of Heaven's resources.

WORSHIP GOD

— Faith is the purest form of worship.

Look to Jesus as the source of everything you need. Walk in the understanding that as you direct your trust toward Him, you are providing pure worship to Him. As you place your trust in Him, you are walking on His path for your life. This path is your destiny. You will find peace, strength, and assurance arising in your heart as you live in your Divine purpose. This increasing faith will be the result of aligning with your created purpose.

GET POSITIONED

— Faith divinely positions us with God.

See yourself correctly positioned with God. Be like Moses and walk with simple meekness before God.

Meekness will express a dependence on God as the source of everything good. This will position you to receive everything good from Him.

Jesus was meek. He was totally dependent on the Father and the power of the Holy Spirit working through Him while He walked on the earth as the "Son of Man." The Father trusted Jesus with Divine power and authority.

Matthew 5:5 NKJV
Blessed are the meek,
For they shall inherit the earth.

Meekness results in our being seated with Jesus. Meekness elevates God above ourselves in our heart. As you elevate God in your heart, He will lift you up to a higher position on the earth.

Matthew 16:17-19 MSG
Jesus came back, "God bless you, Simon, son of Jonah!
You didn't get that answer out of books or from teachers.
My Father in Heaven, God himself, let you in on this secret
of who I really am. And now I'm going to tell you who
you are, really are. You are Peter, a rock. This is the rock on
which I will put together my church, a church so
expansive with energy that not even the
gates of hell will be able to keep it out.

"And that's not all. You will have complete and
free access to God's kingdom, keys to open any and
every door: no more barriers between Heaven and earth,
earth and Heaven. A yes on earth is yes in Heaven.
A no on earth is no in Heaven."

SEE WITH YOUR FAITH

— Faith sees the world as it should be.

Allow God to direct your life as He gives you a vision in your heart. Delight yourself in Him and expect that He will align your desires with His.

He will guide you into a blessed life by placing desires within your heart. These desires will always be in agreement with His standards of Holiness as expressed in the Bible. Allow Him to become the wind in your sail that carries you across life's ocean.

Psalms 37:4 NKJV
Delight yourself also in the LORD,
And He shall give you the desires of your heart.

Philippians 2:13 NKJV
for it is God who works in you both to will and to do
for His good pleasure.

Colossians 3:1-3 MSG
(So if you're serious about living this new resurrection
life with Christ, act like it. Pursue the things over which
Christ presides. Don't shuffle along, eyes to the ground,

> absorbed with the things right in front of you.
> Look up, and be alert to what is going on around
> Christ—that's where the action is. See things from his
> perspective. Your old life is dead. Your new life, which is
> your real life—even though invisible to spectators—
> is with Christ in God. He is your life.

See what God is placing into your heart and allow these to overpower what you currently see in your world. Learn to work with God to shape your world into what He desires.

ENTER INTO REST

— Faith provides rest.

Success depends on entering into His rest. This is achieved by faith. Stop trying to make God love you. Stop trying to do things with your own strength. Believe that God loves you now and that He loves you enough to transform you into His Son's image. He loves you now and forever. Believe that He is doing the work in and through you.

Entering into His rest can only completely happen by being immersed into His Presence. This is known as the Baptism of the Holy Spirit.

Acts 19:1-6 NKJV
And it happened, while Apollos was at Corinth, that Paul,

having passed through the upper regions, came to
Ephesus. And finding some disciples he said to them,
"Did you receive the Holy Spirit when you believed?"

So they said to him, "We have not so much as heard
whether there is a Holy Spirit."

And he said to them,
"Into what then were you baptized?"

So they said, "Into John's baptism."

Then Paul said, "John indeed baptized with a baptism
of repentance, saying to the people that they should
believe on Him who would come after him, that is, on
Christ Jesus."

When they heard this, they were baptized in the name of
the Lord Jesus. And when Paul had laid hands on them,
the Holy Spirit came upon them, and they spoke with
tongues and prophesied.

God can baptize you into the Holy Spirit by more
than one way. One way is to have someone that has
been immersed into the Holy Spirit to pray for you to
receive the same. You can also ask Jesus to baptize you
with the Holy Spirit (Luke 3:16 and John 20:22). He
is very generous with His Spirit after you receive Him
as Savior and Lord.

Having His Presence is the most essential requirement for having a faith that can move mountains. Walking with and yielding to His manifested Presence is the key to becoming like Jesus.

Find people that have been baptized by the Holy Spirit and whose lives match the teachings of Jesus and the Bible. Then hang out with them. Fellowshipping with people that walk in God's Presence will greatly benefit you. That's how Jesus did it. He hung out with His disciples. They received strength and impartation from Jesus by spending time with Him. You can gain strength and impartation from people that are anointed as well.

MOTIVATIONAL INSIGHTS

Don't stop believing!

The most common reason that many people do not come into a powerful faith is that they give up too soon. If you purpose in your mind to live a supernatural life of faith and don't give up, you will receive your desire (Proverbs 10:24).

Jesus taught a parable of what real faith looked like

in the story of a widow who pestered an evil judge for so long that he finally gave in (Luke 18:1-8). We know that God is a good God, and yet Jesus still marveled at this woman's persistence.

In Luke 18:6-8, Jesus said, "*Hear what the unjust judge said. And shall God not avenge His own elect who cry out day and night to Him, though He bears long with them? I tell you that He will avenge them speedily. Nevertheless, when the Son of Man comes, will He really find faith on the earth?*"

We must be determined to never stop believing just because something doesn't happen immediately. Can you imagine that Jesus asked if He would really find faith on the earth when He returned? You will receive if you don't quit!

Use what you have and you will get more.

There is a principle reflected in the Bible about how we can increase in something by using what we have.

Jesus taught that if we use what God has given us, we will receive an increase from Him. In God's Kingdom, a key to growth is to use what you have (see Matthew 25:14-29).

Use your faith to believe in Jesus as your Savior.

This will produce more faith that will produce His life inside of you. Growing in Him produces more faith in your heart.

The more you use your faith, the more you get!

Romans 1:17 AMP
For in the Gospel the righteousness of God is revealed, both springing from faith and leading to faith [disclosed in a way that awakens more faith]. As it is written and forever remains written, "The just and upright shall live by faith.

There are no limits.

The kingdom of God is all about increase. In fact the Bible says, "*Of the increase of His government and peace There will be no end*" (see Isaiah 9:6-7 NKJV). This means that His kingdom is increasing and will always be increasing.

Jesus said that the kingdom of God does not come with observation of external things but is in us (see Luke 17:20-21).

The kingdom of God is righteousness and peace and joy in the Holy Spirit (see Romans 14:16-17 NKJV)! The King's kingdom is inside of us. And of the increase of His government there will be no end.

This means that we should have even more available to us than the early church had. There has been two-thousand years of increase. It's time to believe for it.

Isaiah 9:6-7 NKJV

For unto us a Child is born,
Unto us a Son is given;
And the government will be upon His shoulder.
And His name will be called
Wonderful, Counselor, Mighty God,
Everlasting Father, Prince of Peace.
Of the increase of His government and peace
There will be no end,
Upon the throne of David and over His kingdom,
To order it and establish it with judgment and justice
From that time forward, even forever.
The zeal of the Lord of hosts will perform this.

Paul wrote a letter to the Christians in Corinth giving them insights and direction. Paul wanted them to know that there was no limit to their spiritual growth. He used the story from the Old Testament of how Moses put a veil over his face because he radiated with a bright light after spending time on the mountain with God.

Moses radiated with the Glory of God which produced a shining light from his face. This Glory gradually faded away because God was moving toward His ultimate solution for reconnecting with mankind.

Paul said that the children of Israel still have a veil over their hearts to this day when they read the law. This represents a religious veil that prevents them from seeing His current revealed truth.

There are still religious veils among even some Christians today. Jesus appeared to the apostle John after His resurrection and described Himself: "*I am the Alpha and the Omega, the Beginning and the End,*" says the Lord, "*who is and who was and who is to come, the Almighty.*" (Revelation 1:8 NKJV)

Many believers today don't see Jesus properly, as He is. They worship the one "who was" and look forward to the one "who is to come."

Removing religious veils allows people to behold Jesus as He really is. This connects them to God by His Spirit. People are set free as they abide in God's Presence, the Powerful Person of the Holy Spirit. As we abide in His Presence, we are changed into His image. It is in this manner that we can see Jesus, the One who is.

Communion with Holy Spirit transforms the person from one level to ever higher levels. There is no limit to how much someone can grow spiritually. Paul said that we can go from glory to glory:

2 Corinthians 3:16-18 NKJV

Nevertheless when one turns to the Lord, the veil
is taken away. Now the Lord is the Spirit; and where
the Spirit of the Lord is, there is liberty. But we all,
with unveiled face, beholding as in a mirror the glory
of the Lord, are being transformed into the same image
from glory to glory, just as by the Spirit of the Lord.

There is a generation of people
that will mature to such a point
that they will be like Jesus when
He returns. I don't see any reason
why that generation can't be us.

1 John 3:2 NKJV

Beloved, now we are children of God;
and it has not yet been revealed what we shall be,
but we know that when He is revealed,
we shall be like Him, for we shall see Him as He is.

11

TESTIMONY OF JESUS

Revelation 19:10 NKJV
And I fell at his feet to worship him.
But he said to me, "See that you do not do that!
I am your fellow servant, and of your brethren who
have the testimony of Jesus. Worship God! For the
testimony of Jesus is the spirit of prophecy."

We can overcome by using the testimonies that
Jesus has won for us. Testimonies are stories that testify about Jesus and what He has accomplished. When
we share these stories with people, we are declaring
what is available to them. We are announcing Jesus,
the One who was, the One who is, and the One who
is to come.

Acts 10:34-35 NKJV
Then Peter opened his mouth and said: "In truth
I perceive that God shows no partiality. But in every
nation whoever fears Him and works righteousness
is accepted by Him.

God has made His offer to every single person without exception. What He is willing to do for one person He is willing to do for everyone. Here are a few testimonies of how Jesus has worked in our lives.

VITAMINS FROM HEAVEN

My wife and I overheard a lady named Karen talking about her infirmity with the store employee in the vitamin section. She had severe pain that shot through her back and down her leg. The doctor suspected that it was fibromyalgia. She was looking for herbs or vitamins that could relieve her pain.

We asked Karen if we could pray for her. She said, "At this point I'm willing to try anything." We asked Jesus to heal her and then she said, "I can feel heat… I'm getting hot." I asked how her pain was and she said, "The pain is leaving… It's almost zero."

We prayed again and then I said, "It's done, you're healed now."

She said, "I know I'm healed because I could feel something go down my leg and out the bottom of my left foot!"

Karen was relieved because the pain had been so bad that she was in jeopardy of losing her job. She wasn't a Christian, but she knew that Jesus had healed her and that He loved her.

12 YEARS OF PAIN

My daughter and I went driving around looking for people to pray for. We were near a hotel when we saw a man and woman walking down the street. The woman was limping and appeared to be in pain.

We approached them and said that we believed God wanted us to pray for them. His name was Eli and her name was Lisa. Lisa said, "I'm in pain because of fibromyalgia. I've had it for about 12 years." Her pain level was close to an 8 out of 10.

We asked Jesus to heal her and remove the pain. Suddenly, a strong, cool breeze blew through, which all of us noticed. I asked how her pain was. Lisa said, "My pain level has decreased." Then she quickly looked at Eli and said, "There's no pain!" She began to walk around and said, "I can walk more freely now, and there is no pain!"

We asked Eli if he needed prayer. He said that he was schizophrenic and bipolar. I told him that Jesus would heal him. We prayed for him, and another strong cool breeze blew through us as we prayed. Eli said, "I felt something leave my head, and I feel lighter."

Eli and Lisa were excited and happy as they left. Jesus is wonderful!

A DAY IN THE PARK

I went walking in a park early in the morning. Two young ladies were walking ahead of me. The Lord revealed to me that one of them had hip pain. I caught up to them and asked if I could pray for them. With an expression of surprise they introduced themselves as Samantha and Felicia. I said, "The Lord wants me to pray for you, Samantha. Do you have pain in the hip or legs?"

She said, "I have pain in my hip and back."

We asked Jesus to heal her. The pain totally left her back, and the pain in her hip had diminished to almost nothing. She started weeping and said she had scoliosis. I said, "Do something you couldn't do before."

She bent over and touched the ground. She exclaimed, "That! I couldn't do that!"

Then I looked at Felicia and said, "I believe the Lord has something He wants me to tell you… but I'm still waiting to hear what it is." They seemed nervous as we stood there for what seemed like a long time. Then I said, "The Lord says… That which you have been longing for has arrived." They were stunned as they both began to weep.

Felicia said, "If you knew what we were just talking about you would know why we're crying." Just before I walked up, they were talking about their circle of friends and all that they had been going through. Felicia had just said, "I long for the time when we could all be walking with the Lord together."

FLOWER POWER

After a high school event, my daughter received a bouquet of yellow roses which we placed on our dining room table. After a week, they had wilted over and grown brown around the edges. My daughter didn't want to get rid of them, so we kept them there.

Shortly after, we were all gathered in another room praying for a family member to be healed. After praying, we all went into the living room. My daughter had mentioned that it felt like there was something electric in the air.

Suddenly, we looked toward the dining room and on the table was a beautiful bouquet of fresh yellow roses! They were bigger than before, too. The flowers had been restored.

This was one of the first supernatural occurrences

that my daughter witnessed. It showed her that God was good at restoring life to any circumstance.

ADVENTURES AT THE DEPARTMENT STORE

Leaving the department store, we noticed a lady working as a greeter who had her arm in a sling. We asked what happened.

She had broken her arm just below her shoulder two weeks earlier. The doctors could not put her arm in a cast due to the location of the break. Her pain level was at a 5, and she could not lift her arm. We asked if we could pray for her and she said, "Yes!"

After a brief prayer, we asked her to try it out. Her eyes got big as she said, "It doesn't hurt. I can move it now! Now I will be able to do my exercises!" All the pain went away, and she could lift her arm up high.

Jesus is really good!

HELPING RHONDA

We saw a lady limping near the mall. After introducing ourselves, we asked if we could pray for her. She said, "My name is Rhonda and I'm in pain because of cerebral palsy." In her forties, Rhonda said she had not been without severe pain for many years.

We asked Jesus to heal her, then a strong, cool breeze swirled around us. All the pain left her body!

She said, "All my muscles relaxed, and I don't weeble-wobble when I walk now!"

Rhonda came up to us a few weeks later in the mall. She looked wonderful. She said, "I just wanted to say 'Hello' and to tell you that I'm still doing great."

MIRACLE IN THE LAUNDROMAT

My daughter and I went to a laundromat to pray for people. Inside we met a woman named Velma who had a goiter larger than a golf ball. The goiter caused a large bulge at the base of her neck. She was scheduled for surgery to have her thyroid removed soon. We asked Jesus to heal her.

Within seconds, the large bulge began to shrink right under my fingers. She reached up to feel her neck and was surprised that the goiter was gone! Her daughter-in-law looked with surprise and confirmed that the goiter was gone.

BROKEN ELBOW

My daughter and I saw Emilio riding his bike with one hand down a busy street. Later we found out that he had broken his elbow the previous week. His arm was in a soft splint and body sling.

We turned into a parking lot just as he fell over onto the ground, landing on his injured elbow. He was in agony to the point of barely being able to speak when we approached him.

We asked Jesus to heal him, and within seconds all the pain was gone! He began to openly weep with joy as he flexed his hand and moved his arm. He said, "All the pain is gone!"

Jesus had removed the pain and healed his elbow.

OUT OF THE WHEELCHAIR!

We saw Debra being pushed in her wheelchair along a busy downtown street by her friend. She had been hit by a car two months earlier. The doctors tried to rebuild her right knee, but she was unable to walk or stand. She said, "I suffer from depression, and I have been in severe pain since the surgery. I can't bend my left knee at all. I don't think I will ever be able to walk again."

We asked Jesus to heal her. She instantly went unconscious and fell forward, almost falling out of her wheelchair. I caught her by placing my hand on her forehead. We were stunned and didn't really know what to do. I stood there holding her up for a few seconds as people stared at us as they drove by. Then I said, "In Jesus' name I command your spirit to sit up." Debra was not conscience and yet, with her eyes still closed and her head hanging down, she slowly sat straight up in the chair!

After a few moments, she slowly opened her eyes and started laughing with great joy. Debra said, "I feel better! The pain is gone!"

I asked if she wanted to try to stand and she said, "Yes!" She grabbed my elbow and stood right up. She began to slowly walk while shouting with joy, "I'm walking! I can bend my leg!"

Debra just kept walking and shouting, "I'm walking! I can bend my leg and the pain is gone!"

About this time, a police officer pulled up and asked if she needed assistance. I said, "It's okay, Jesus just healed her."

He looked at us and sarcastically quipped, "Praise the Lord." The officer then turned to Debra and asked if she needed assistance.

She said, "No, Jesus just healed me!"

Then the officer said, "Say, aren't you the ones that sell papers over at the intersection?"

Debra nodded and said, "Yes, that's us."

After a minute or two, the officer looked at Debra and said, "Now how long ago were you hit?"

His demeanor had changed from cool skepticism to warm interest. An ambulance pulled up with lights flashing shortly after the police officer left. Two paramedics approached and repeated the same conversation we had with the police officer. Debra told them again that Jesus had healed her, so they left as well. Jesus is really good!

I LOVE LUCY

One day the Lord led me to a building with a sign that read, "Free Tax Preparation." There was a very long line of people waiting outside. I felt the Lord tell me to go pray for someone in the line.

I parked my car and walked along the line of people asking if anyone needed healing. I started at the end and worked my way toward the front. I walked along a few people at a time and asked, "Does anyone need prayer for healing?" They just shook their heads no, snickered, or ignored me.

Once I got near the front of the line, I stopped and asked if anyone there needed prayer for healing. I heard someone to my left chuckle. All the people got quiet and just looked at me. So I asked again, "Does anyone need prayer for healing? I believe the Lord has sent me here."

Then an older woman standing right in front of me raised her hand and in a timid voice said, "Me… I do.

My name is Lucy and I have back pain. It hurts just standing here."

By now we had the attention of everyone in line. All the people stood quietly watching to see what would happen next.

I asked Jesus to heal Lucy. She said, "The pain is all gone!" She twisted from side to side and said "No pain!" Lots of people got to see Jesus demonstrate His power and love for Lucy.

MORE THAN WE COULD ASK OR THINK

My daughter and I saw a man named Marcello walking along the road. The Lord directed us to stop and pray for him. I asked if he needed prayer. He said he was in severe pain and had been walking a long distance. Marcello explained that he had broken his right leg twenty years earlier, and the doctors had inserted a steel rod in his femur in an effort to save his leg. He walked with a limp and had been in pain all those years.

I asked if he could stand on his toes and he responded, "No." We asked what else he needed prayer for. He said that he had injured his right shoulder six years earlier. It has caused severe pain since then, and he was not able to work due to the injury.

We asked the Lord Jesus to heal him. Then we asked Marcello to try his shoulder out. His eyes grew large as he lifted his arm and moved his shoulder. He said, "The pain is gone. I couldn't do that!"

Then I asked him to try his leg. He looked with amazement as he walked around and said, "There's no pain!" Then I asked him to try to stand on his toes. Looking at us with a smile, he went right up on his toes!

Marcello looked at us and said, "I had a terrible tooth pain and it is even gone!" He had severe pain in a tooth, but he didn't mention it to us. The Lord knew and healed that, too!

TAKE A KNEE

One day we were driving with a family friend named Jerin and looking for people to pray for. We saw a young man walking with a limp toward some apartments. He had a black leg brace on his right knee. We pulled over and asked him if we could pray for him and he said, "Yes."

The man, whose name was Toby, told us he had reconstructive surgery within the last four weeks due to a torn ACL in his knee. His pain level was very high, and he was not able to walk without pain. He also could not fully extend his knee.

We prayed for Toby in Jesus' name, and immediately he said he felt better and was able to walk and flex his knee without pain!

Suddenly he removed his knee brace and vigorously started doing deep knee bends. He shook his head in shock as he walked back and forth. Then he showed us the large scar in the shape of a cross on his knee from the surgery.

He told us that he had just recently believed in Jesus as his savior and had been baptized the week before. This encounter demonstrated the kind of loving God he had given his heart to.

SUNDAY IN THE PARK

Several of us went to the park to do ministry one Sunday morning. We were sitting at a picnic table under a pavilion as an older man rode up on a bike and sat at the same table. This seemed odd because there were three other available tables near us.

I asked, "Do you need prayer?"

He said, "Maybe."

We asked him his name and why he needed prayer. His name was Roberto, and he had severe back pain because he had two screws put in his spine after being hit by a car a few years ago.

We asked Jesus to remove the screws and to restore his spine. I asked how he felt on a scale of 1 to 10.

Roberto said, "It's better… maybe a 6." We prayed again and he said, "The pain is less… maybe a 2." Then we prayed again. He was weeping as he looked up and said, "The pain has gone… a zero!"

He was homeless due to not being able to work after his accident. We prayed that he would get a job and a home. He said he would be able to work now that the pain was gone.

All of these things are available to you. Make a decision to follow Jesus and HE will do the impossible through you!

Endnotes

[1] Matthew 21:21-22
[2] John 14:12
[3] Matthew 18:3
[4] John 11:40
[5] Luke 12:48
[6] Romans 2:11-16
[7] Romans 5:14-17
[8] Romans 12:3
[9] Ephesians 2:8-9
[10] John 3:16
[11] Exodus 20:4-5
[12] 1 John 4:8
[13] 1 Corinthians 1:9
[14] 1 John 4:19
[15] 1 Timothy 1:18-19
[16] Romans 1:21
[17] 1 John 1:9
[18] Romans 5:20-21
[19] 1 Peter 1:15-16
[20] Ephesians 2:4-7
[21] 1 Thessalonians 2:13
[22] Exodus 3:14
[23] Romans 14:20-23
[24] Exodus 20:8-11
[25] Hebrews 3:19
[26] Hebrews 4:9-10
[27] John 19:30
[28] 2 Corinthians 5:17
[29] Matthew 10:7-8
[30] Ephesians 2:1-2

LASTING LIBERTY
MINISTRIES

For more information or
for prayer requests
visit us at *lastingliberty.org*.

LASTING LIBERTY MINISTRIES
P.O. Box 1371
Wolfforth, TX 79382